MISCARRIAGE of JUSTICE

MISCARRIAGE of JUSTICE

An Irish Family's Story of
Wrongful Conviction as IRA Terrorists

ANNE MAGUIRE
with
Jim Gallagher

Introduction by
Elizabeth Shannon

Foreword by
Cardinal Basil Hume

Roberts Rinehart Publishers

Published in the US and Canada by Roberts Rinehart Publishers,
P.O. Box 666, Niwot, Colorado 80544
Distributed by Publishers Group West

Anne Maguire and Jim Gallagher assert the moral right
to be identified as the authors of this work

First published in Great Britain in 1994 by HarperCollins Publishers

ISBN 1–57098–006–3

Library of Congress Catalog Card Number 94-67993

Set in Janson Text 12/15pt

Typesetting:
Red Barn Publishing, Skeagh, Skibbereen, Co. Cork, Ireland

Printed in the United States of America

This book is dedicated to four people: Mary and Hugh McCaffrey along with my Aunt Teasy and late Uncle Bill.

And to my husband Paddy, our three sons and daughter. I thank them with all my heart for keeping our family bond intact and strong. It is more precious to me than anything.

FOREWORD

Recently I listened to Anne Maguire speaking to close on two hundred young people. As she told her story they listened to her quite spellbound. It was not so much her story, immensly disquieting as this is, but the quality of the lady who was speaking which impressed them. It was her dignity, her evident goodness and the total lack of bitterness which spoke more eloquently than her words. Anne Maguire has now put her story into print and I believe that the reading of this book will make a profound impression on readers as it did on the young people as they listened to her speaking.

Anne Maguire was caught up in a terrible situation not of her making, accused unjustly of a crime she never committed.

To have met her and to have sat with her in conversation adds to the total improbability of her or any of her family being involved in the terrible crimes of which she was accused.

Anne Maguire never lost her faith in God and in humanity. Perhaps it took this ordeal to bring the best out of her, and she is, as far as I am concerned, a very exceptional woman whom it has been a privilege to get to know.

Basil Hume
Archbishop of Westminster
27 October 1993

INTRODUCTION

I met Anne Maguire at her home in Maida Vale, a tree-lined neighborhood of London, on a warm June morning. The street was filled with women pushing prams, children playing, two young Bobbys walking slowly side by side, all creating a pretty, placid, and safe London scene.

In the living room of her small house, Anne was expertly feeding her six-month-old grandson while other children and grandchildren wandered in and out. One could easily think: "All's right with the world" here. But that world went terribly wrong for Anne Maguire and her family in December 1974, when a series of events began to unroll which would end as an eleven-year nightmare for Anne, her husband and her two sons. They became the innocent victims of a terrible and frightening miscarriage of British justice and spent harrowing, humiliating years in prison before their innocence was established. So intense was the political pressure to find terrorists that the police were determined to find their prey, whether innocent or guilty.

On that December day, Anne's nephew, Gerard Conlon, along with his friend, Paul Hill, was arrested on suspicion of involvement with the bombing of the Guildford pub. During his brutal interrogation, Conlon gave Anne's name to the police as a relative in London, someone he knew and had previously stayed with. That connection was all that was needed to send police and sniffer dogs to the Maguire home, haul Anne, her husband Paddy, her thirteen-year-old son Patrick, her fifteen-year-old son John, and her sixteen-year-old son Vincent off to a police station where another brutal interrogation began. Anne was abused physically and verbally, kicked and beaten, called a "murdering Irish bastard," and finally accused of murder.

Anne and Paddy Maguire were held on remand awaiting their trial, which began in January 1976. On March 3, the jury returned "guilty" verdicts and Anne and her husband were sentenced to fourteen years in prison. Their son Vincent received five years, and thirteen-year-old Patrick got four years.

Separated from her family, including her eight-year-old daughter, Anne-Marie, Anne Maguire began serving her sentence in Durham jail, which was to be her home for the next seven years.

The doting mother who used to do five cleaning jobs to help support her family, her husband (a former soldier in the British Army), one son who wanted to grow up and join the British Army and another who wanted to join the police—innocent all—went off to jail on trumped-up charges.

On February 22, 1985, after having served nine years, Anne Maguire was released. The other members of her family were already free. Anne began the long road of re-adjustment to her new life out of prison, becoming re-acquainted with her beloved daughter, Anne-Marie, whose childhood she lost, and her grandchildren. She and Paddy, separated for so long, had to learn to share each other's lives again. Patrick is in therapy, scarred from his years in an adult prison.

Anne is not bitter, nor is she full of recriminations for all those who were responsible for the destruction of eleven years of her life. As she sat that June morning in her neat little house in Maida Vale, her innate dignity, goodness and strength of character were apparent in everything she said. Her dark eyes shone with humor as she recounted some of the stories from the days in prison.

"They sent a representative around from the Home Office to interview me, and she spoke to me in Irish. I suppose they were real proud of having someone with that skill. I had to say 'Sorry, luv, but I don't speak a word of Irish myself'!"

"Forgive us our trespasses as we forgive those who trespass against us," is Anne's philosophy and one that she finds it possible to practice. Her deeply-held religious beliefs were central to keeping her well while in prison and free of hate and bitterness upon her release. She does, however, feel frustration at the manner in which she and her family were portrayed in the movie, *In the Name of the Father*, which told the story of the Guildford Four.

"Paul Hill was never in my house," she reflected. "And there were so many other distortions. I wish that Jim Sheridan (the director) had come to see me before he made the movie instead of afterwards. My son Patrick said to him: "*My Left Foot* is a brilliant movie, but you made *In the Name of the Father* with your left foot!"

In December 1992, Sir John May, who led the inquiry into the Guildford bombings, produced his report on the 'Maguire Seven,' and called it the worst miscarriage of justice he had ever seen.

The Maguires have yet to receive full compensation for the years they spent in prison.

The British government has never apologized to the Maguire family for the terrible injustice done to them.

Elizabeth Shannon
Boston
26 June 1994

PREFACE

Many people, both 'on the inside' in prison and since my release, have asked me how I coped with being separated from my family and with wrongful imprisonment. How did I keep my sanity?

I think there were three reasons why I did not submit to utter despair.

God was on my side. My faith was, and is, the most important thing. Others can take away your freedom, your family, or your possessions, but no one can take your faith from you. My faith in God kept me going. It made me strong when I was weak. It led me to believe that one day there would be light at the end of the tunnel.

Peace of mind. Despite all the sufferings or anguish, at least I had peace of mind where it really mattered. I had a clear conscience. I knew I had committed no crime.

Forgiveness. From the beginning I forgave those who falsely implicated us, those who wrongly convicted, imprisoned and maltreated us. This was my strength. Without it I would be a sick woman. 'Forgive us our trespasses as we forgive those who trespass against us.'

I would like to thank the following people who, in one way or another, helped me and my family to come through: George Basil Cardinal Hume, Archbishop of Westminster; Sister Sarah Clarke; Alastair and Pat Logan, our solicitors and our friends; Robert Kee; Fr Faul; Fr McKinley; Fr McKenna, HMP Durham; Fr Bobby Gilmore, Fr Paddy Smith and Nuala Kelly of the Irish Commission for Prisoners Overseas; Rt Revd Monsignor Buckley; the late Cardinal O'Fiach; Mr and the late Mrs Atkison, our neighbours on Third Avenue; Rt Hon Merlyn Rees; Lords Fitt, Longford, Jenkins, Scarman and Devlin; Sir John Wheeler, MP; the late Sir John Biggs-Davison; John Hume, MP; Christopher Price, MP; the MPs of all parties who signed Early Day Motion No. 280 (Miscarriage of Justice); Grant McKee; Ross Franey; Tom McGurk; Joe Mulholland, Pat Cox and Liam O'Flanagan of RTE; Professor Mary McAleese of Queen's University; Chief Prison Officer Mona Clough, PO Joan Barr, PO Chris Gibson, PO V. Brown, all of HMP Durham; Sean Smyth and Pat O'Neil; Mrs Teresa Roache and family; Leila and Billy O'Brien and family; Mr and Mrs Metcalfe; Fred Kemp; Mr and Mrs S. F. Irvine; Mr and Mrs Willie McCann; Mr and Mrs Hugh Maguire; Sean Tully and family; Olive Maguire; Mr and Mrs Joe Hoey; Mrs Nan Turner and family; Mrs Bridget Hughes; Kathy and Eileen Cullinane; Martin Rogers; Fr Murray and the late Fr Brady of Belfast; Fr Jerry Reynolds of Clonard Monastery and other family and friends too numerous to mention; Anne and Eileen, Judy and Carole, Sally Allen, Liz Thomson, Anne Merchant and others who befriended me in prison and helped me through my sentence; all those people in so many different parts of the world who sent cards and letters to me and my family while in prison and also during our campaign. Their support and prayers meant a lot to us.

ONE

I was born Anne Smyth in the Falls Road area of Belfast on 14 November 1935. My parents were living in the front bedroom of a house at 1 Oakman Street with my sister Mary, who is eleven months older than me. They would have eight children in all; five boys and three girls. I am the second eldest.

After I was born my parents moved to Abyssinia Street, off Leesson Street in the Falls Road. That is where we all lived and grew up. My father only moved out of there into new flats in the early 1980s. The house was 'two up, two down.' The toilet was out in the yard, and there was no bathroom. (We were bathed in a big tub in front of the coal fire.) There were no washing machines or any of the mod cons we have today. My mother did her washing by hand on the old scrubbing board. She also baked a lot of her own bread and cakes.

Mother's parents lived nearby and my grandmother ran a fish and chip shop from her house. Even though Mummy had all of us to cope with, she helped out my grandmother a couple of days a week as fish-fryer, to supplement my father's wages. He worked on a coal cart with the local coalman, Leo Healey. The pay would not have been all that good, but Mummy and Daddy brought us up to the best of their abilities, as I myself have tried to do with my children. They did not have much but it seemed plenty. There were certainly other kids worse off than we were. Mummy was always able to get us something made out of old trousers or other cast-offs. Our next-door neighbour, Nellie Bramble, made trousers for the boys and another neighbour made dresses for us girls.

In Abyssinia Street, and I am sure all over Belfast, neighbours were not just neighbours. We were all like one big extended family. People helped each other and there was a strong community spirit.

Leesson Street and the Falls Road was a Catholic area of Belfast. It was actually known as a Republican area (that is the Catholic population of the area would support a return to a United Ireland), but that doesn't mean that every person who lived there supported the IRA. In our house politics were not discussed. My father's concern was whether we had done our homework, learned our catechism and said our prayers.

Mummy was not a churchgoer but she believed in God and used to say to us, 'If you can't do a good turn for someone, don't do them a bad turn. Always try to help, no matter how little.' And that's the way she lived herself. If she knew of any family in need, she would immediately cut the loaf of bread in half and send one of us to deliver it, along with a pot of soup or stew. When she died at the age of fifty-four, the local priest said she was a saint because he knew how much she had done to help others. Daddy was a churchgoer and would take us to Mass, encouraged and supported by Mummy. She wanted us to receive our First Holy Communion, be confirmed and grow up with religious values.

Like everyone else in the area, I went to the local schools, first the primary on Leesson Street—'wee

Leessie' we used to call it—and then on to the secondary, St Peter's on Raglan Street. I loved school and in our last year at primary my friends and I would go in and help the mistresses with the infants—'the babies' we called them. I enjoyed secondary school too—most of all the cookery classes and essay-writing. I was no good at drawing or art, no matter how hard I tried. The needlework classes were also a nightmare because I knew I needed glasses and couldn't see properly to do the close work. I used to beg my mother to let me stay at home on those days saying, 'Mummy, if you let me stay home I'll scrub the house from top to bottom for you!' It was to no avail.

My sister Mary and I, being the eldest, had our household chores to do. Mummy believed that as girls we should learn to scrub floors, make beds, and generally keep house. From the age of seven or eight, she would put a little apron on us, give us a bucket of water and scrubbing brush, and tell us to scrub down the outside step. It certainly did us no harm. Rather, it did us good, because once you have your own family you are able to cope. As we got older, Mary would clean upstairs and I would do downstairs. Mummy cleaned as well, and also did the cooking and the washing. I think when we were young she let us do our cleaning chores, but once we had gone out she would have to go over them properly herself. She was letting us know that as girls we would have to do this as we got older.

I knew I needed glasses but would not give in to the fact. After all, people who wore glasses were called all sorts of names. It was only after the birth of my third child in 1961, when my eyesight deteriorated even further, that I finally gave in and got a pair of spectacles. Even then I wouldn't wear them all the time, only when

I had to read something, like the prices on the supermarket shelves. Back on the street, I would slip them into my pocket. Oh vanity!

I would like to have stayed on at school and then gone to Orange's Academy for senior pupils. Miss Orange had told me I had the ability and would be accepted. But, being the second eldest of the family, Mummy needed me to go out to work. So at the age of fourteen I left school. At that time in our area, people went either to the mills or, for the majority, to the wareroom, the factory. Not many people from our area got good jobs, being Catholic. You just didn't, even if you had the qualifications. Your religion counted against you, which was a sorry state of affairs.

Our neighbour, Nellie Bramble, found me a place in the wareroom with her, making army tunics and uniforms. With my poor eyesight I didn't greatly enjoy it. One day the supervisor kept on and on at us to work harder and faster, I knew that I could hardly see what I was supposed to be sewing as I needed glasses, so I just stood up and announced I was leaving and would not be coming back. I was a bit of a tomboy in my younger days and would tackle anything. My sister Mary was much more refined than I. If a boy had hit me, I would have hit him back. When I went home and told Mummy I had left the job, she tried to persuade me to go back. It was a trade, she said, and one day I would have a husband and sons of my own and would be able to make them trousers and suits and earn some money into the bargain. But I was adamant. I was not going back and anyway, I was never going to get married! That was me at fourteen. But her words came true and I do regret not having stuck out the job.

Another good neighbour, Josie Campbell (née Rae), got me a job in the weaving at Elliot's on the Springfield

Road. She taught me how to use the loom. Mary was already working there. It was a great big noisy mill but I loved it and enjoyed the work. Soon, I was operating two looms and earning more money as a result. We started at eight in the morning and finished at six in the evening with a lunch break between noon and half past one. A few of my friends also worked there and we all walked in together. At six o'clock we poured out of the factory gates, home to have our tea. By seven o'clock we would be in the park for a game of camogie, the traditional Irish sport (the girls equivalent of hurling) resembling hockey. Six nights a week I either played camogie or went swimming, depending on the season. From there we would usually go on to the Clonard picture house, where my boyfriend Paddy and his mates would be waiting for us. They would be in before us and keep our seats. We always took up the same two rows, his friends and my friends, and all went around together.

One night a week, though, we didn't go straight home for tea. Thursday was the night of the very popular novena service to Our Lady Mother of Perpetual Help, and the workers' service was at six o'clock. On those nights we would cut across Ornmore Street to the Clonard Monastery for the service. We enjoyed it and certainly weren't pushed to go. When we wanted special favours we would pray to Our Lady of Perpetual Help. If you had fallen out with your boyfriend you would pray, 'Please let him talk to me tonight'—silly, almost childish things like that. It was all innocent. Sex never entered my mind and I had been going out with Paddy since I was fourteen. I never prayed, 'Don't let me weaken,' or anything like that. It was rather, 'Don't let me fall out with him tonight.' Those were my childish prayers and I laugh now when I look back on them.

5

One day the foreman in the mill came over to my sister Mary and told her she had to go home, she was wanted. Why hadn't he asked me? Mary was only eleven months older than me. I remember now that I didn't even know my mother was pregnant.

When the six o'clock whistle blew that night I was out of those gates like a shot and straight home to see what was going on. Mummy always had the table set and the dinner ready, but that night as I burst into the kitchen there was nothing prepared, only Daddy pacing up and down smoking, the ashtray already overflowing. Why was there no tea and where was Mummy? Then I heard the cry of a baby, shot upstairs and burst into Mummy's room. All I could focus on was District Nurse Owens holding this tiny little baby. Mummy shouted 'Get her out' and I ran back downstairs. Shortly afterwards Mary came to fetch a kettle of water and told us Mummy had a baby boy, my youngest brother Robert.

The excitement did not stop me keeping my usual rendezvous at the cinema that night. I couldn't wait to tell the gang my news. When I went in I said, 'Hey fellas, you'll never guess what I got for my tea tonight—a baby brother!' Paddy still brings that up and laughs today. In retrospect I wonder if I was selfish not knowing my mother was pregnant; she must have felt off-colour some days. I suppose I had been protected. But she was quite a stout woman and I honestly did not see any difference. I suppose if she had said she was not feeling well or had a headache I would have tried to help her more.

My boyfriend, Paddy Maguire, was three years older than me. He was my first and only boyfriend.

He joined the army when he was eighteen, going on nineteen. I was sixteen and shed buckets of tears when he left. I wouldn't go out to the cinema any more.

Friends would call round for me but I refused to go out, remaining faithful to Paddy though I still played in our regular camogie matches. He was posted to England and then to Cyprus and we exchanged letters faithfully every week. At the age of eighteen I left the weaving to get a job in the Royal Victoria Hospital, where my sister Mary was already working.

One Sunday lunchtime we had the radio on and a record request came over the airwaves from Paddy Maguire for Annie Smyth in Belfast. It was 'Love letters in the sand.' Ah, young love!

CHAPTER

TWO

When Paddy was posted back to England, he was able to come over to Belfast for the occasional long weekend or week's leave. We got engaged before he was demobbed, and he had been out of the army for about a year when we decided to get married—on 26 September 1957.

He was still living in England along with his brother Hugh, but we agreed to marry in Belfast. Father McConville married us in St Peter's pro-cathedral, our local parish church. I had Mary's wedding dress, just altered a bit. Mary and her husband Hugh McCaffrey paid for the cars. Paddy's sisters Bridget and Sarah bought the wedding cake, and my brother Sean the photo album. My parents, assisted by Mary, Hugh, Paddy and myself, paid for the hotel where we entertained about a hundred guests.

That was on a Thursday, and on the same day we sailed for England. I was the first of the family ever to leave home, and of course there were tearful farewells to the young Annie setting off for this big country so far away! Although I was twenty-one by then, I was still a very young and innocent twenty-one. I had never been outside Belfast, except when we were briefly evacuated to Derry during the war. Paddy had said we would both go over to England, work hard for a year or so, and save enough money to put a deposit on a house back in Belfast. I have lived in London ever since—except for my time in jail, that is.

We arrived in London that night. Paddy didn't think the accommodation he had found for us was quite up to scratch to receive his new bride, so some friends, May Brown and her daughters, were cleaning it out first. Believe it or not, the first night of my marriage I spent with my Aunt Teasy!

The next day Paddy came to collect me and take me to our new home in Larnock Road, Maida Vale. It was one room with a shared cooker out on the landing. When I saw it I burst into tears. We may have lived in a little 'two up, two down' in Belfast, but it was a mansion compared to this. What had happened to the London of my dreams, the London I saw in the picture house, the London where all the movie stars lived? Tearfully I wailed that I wanted to go home. Paddy tried to console me, telling me we would progress to a better flat in time.

Mummy had already sent our wedding presents over before us in a trunk, so I unpacked and began to spread our little bits and pieces around the place. The same day I went out with May Brown and bought some rugs which I scattered around the room. Before long, the place began to take on a more homely air.

We had only been there a couple of months when I spotted an advertisement for a basement flat to let in Maida Vale. The rent was £3.10.0 (£3.50) and we were already paying £3 for our little room. There and then I determined we were going to have it. I called at the address with May Brown and the landlady showed us around. It was heaven! It had a coal fire, a separate kitchen, even a door onto its own little garden. Ideal! I said right away that I would take it and we moved in within a couple of days. Ever since then, except for when I first came out of prison, we have always been lucky enough to live in accommodation with a little garden.

The landlady, Mrs Luppin, became like a second mother to me. She saw that I was not yet working and proposed that I help her in the house. It would pay our rent. Paddy and I agreed it would be a good idea. As a young wife still trying to adjust to life in the big city, and still missing her own mother and family, Mrs Luppin was a great comfort to me. Her whole house was let out in flats, and every morning we would do the cleaning. Then, after a light lunch which we took together, we would head down to Church Street Market to do some shopping.

I began to be sick in the mornings and couldn't understand what was wrong with me. Even though I had been going out with Paddy all those years and we were now man and wife, I was still very bashful (and naive) and didn't know why I had not had my monthly period. One day Mrs Luppin remarked that I was looking a little off-colour and asked if I was feeling all right. I told her about my sickness then went on to tell her I hadn't had my period and was very worried; did she think I could have cancer? No doubt tongue in cheek, she said she didn't think I had cancer, and took me to see her own GP, Dr Elizabeth Wright, who told me I was at least two months pregnant.

I couldn't get home quickly enough to tell Paddy. The hours seemed to stretch as I waited for him to come home from work. I always had the table set and the house as nice as possible with all the pride of a young wife wanting to please her husband. We used to eat our dinner at a table in front of the fire. That evening I said to him, 'Well, you'll never guess what's happened, Paddy.

I'm going to have a baby.' He replied, 'Oh really?' I said he didn't seem very surprised or excited. 'Well, Anne, I could have told you that,' he said and burst into laughter.

That was Vincent, our first boy. All through my pregnancy, even though Mrs Luppin was so good to me, I still wanted to go home. I had left Belfast, but part of my heart remained there. I loved the place, or rather the people. To me, Belfast people are the best in the world—both 'sides'—they are great people. Paddy used to say to me that a great big plane left every hour and a big boat every night. If I wanted to go, I could. But he would not go back there. He would say there was no work over there for him and things were much better in London for our child, with more opportunities. But I couldn't see that. I thought I could get my old job back in the Victoria Hospital and that he would surely find a job. In truth it wasn't really a question of the work; Paddy just did not want to go back there to live.

Vincent was born on the eighth of the eighth '58—in the old St Mary's Hospital on the Harrow Road. We both nearly died. I had been in labour a very long time and the priest was even called out to give me the last rites. Dr Wright came too and in the end I had to have a Caesarean section. When they took the baby away from me, he was a bluey-black colour and Dr Wright gave him the kiss of life. Thereafter she always referred to him as 'her boy.' Thank God, both Vincent and I got over our ordeal.

Mr and Mrs Luppin had no children of their own and doted on the new baby. I continued working for them to pay the rent. Paddy was working in car paintspraying and his wages were not so good. At the top of nearby Randolph Avenue there was a barrow selling fruit and flowers. Every Friday evening Paddy would

11

come down the street carrying a bunch of flowers behind his back—never in front of him, always behind his back! He was always like that. Even right up until we were arrested, Paddy would take Anne-Marie, our youngest, out and they would buy me a bunch of flowers or a box of chocolates.

Eleven months after Vincent's birth, although I was warned not to have any more children for a while, I became pregnant with our second child. John's was a normal birth, in 1959. The next year I was taking the two boys home for a holiday in Belfast to see the family. I was feeling a bit sick again. I had intended to stay with Mummy and Daddy for two weeks, but when I told Mummy I thought I was expecting another baby, she was adamant that I was not going back to a one-bedroomed flat with three children. So I stayed on in Belfast and poor Paddy was left alone at the Luppins'. Eventually he gave that up and moved into a single room while he searched for a bigger flat that we could afford. Our third son, Patrick, was born in March 1961 in Belfast, the only one to be born in Ireland. In fact it was Mummy who gave him his name. She insisted I should call him Patrick Joseph after his father, while I had wanted to name him something like Gary or Kevin. I think it was the only thing son-in-law and mother-in-law ever agreed on!

Paddy found a bigger flat in April, on St Luke's Road, near the Portobello Road. I travelled back with the two boys and the new baby, and Paddy and our good friend Pat O'Neil met us off the boat. As the new flat was costing us £6 in rent, Pat moved in as our lodger. He had a folding bed in the sitting-room.

The landlady's husband was in prison, for robbery I think. The flat was part-furnished, and with her permission I gradually got rid of what was there and replaced it with bits and pieces we bought ourselves. As my mother and the other women in Belfast had taken great pride in 'having their windows nice,' with curtains matching other fabrics, I did the same and made our first real home as attractive as possible. The landlady asked if I would take on the job of collecting the rents from the other tenants in return for a reduction in our own rent. Being like my grandmother, I think, I didn't turn down the opportunity to earn a shilling! We had been there for a couple of years when the landlady's husband returned. He came to visit us and thank us for helping his wife while he was away, fell in love with our basement flat and what we had done with it, and said he and his wife would like to move back into it! He said he would go to the Paddington Churches Housing Association and ask them to re-house us.

I went with a neighbour to the Housing Association and they handed me two sets of keys. One was for a top-floor flat, the other for another basement flat in Tavistock Crescent. When we walked in there, you would have thought someone had riddled the walls with a machine gun. There were holes everywhere! Someone had started trying to put in a fireplace and it was a mess.

However, the rent was just over £2 and we had been paying more than £6 for the previous flat. We moved in and soon had the place ship-shape with the help of a friend who was a decorator. The boys loved their new home. Patrick was still a toddler but the older two were thrilled at the trains passing the bottom of the garden from Westbourne Park tube station. We were there until our fourth child, Anne-Marie, was born and the Council took over from Paddington Churches. Anne-Marie was born in October 1966. Mummy had taken the oldest two boys, Vincent and John, over to Belfast to give me a rest. Patrick used to say he would not leave his mummy because he was buying a little sister. Every week I took him with me when I went to have my check-up at Saints John and Elizabeth's Hospital in St John's Wood. It was a private hospital run by nuns which took two non-paying patients. Nobody knew the difference but, needless to say, I was one of them. After every visit, I used to give little Patrick some money to put in the collecting box at the door, and the nun on duty used to say to him that it wouldn't be long now until he had a new baby sister. Patrick got the not-illogical idea into his little head that if he kept putting money into the box, he would soon have paid up enough for a little sister! I used to pray to myself, 'Lord, let it be a girl, or he'll want to know why!'

As my delivery date grew nearer, Mummy brought the two older boys back and stayed to look after them and Paddy when I went into hospital. She used to say to me she would die happy when she saw me having a daughter and my own house—a real house. I used to ask her in return if she had any idea how difficult it was to get an actual house in London. Anyway, Mummy did see my little daughter Anne-Marie who was born on 7 October 1966.

Once we were back home again she returned to Belfast, but promised that she would come back to visit us again after Christmas. It was not to be. Mummy suffered a stroke and went into a coma that Christmas Eve. I remember clearly her last day in London. It was a lovely autumn afternoon in October. I remarked to Paddy how the sun seemed to catch her hair, there seemed to be such a glow about her.

Before she left the flat, I came into the kitchen after feeding the baby to find Mummy sitting with her three

14

little grandsons. She was teaching them the hymn 'All things bright and beautiful.' It is a lovely last memory to have of my mother, singing with her grandchildren, 'The Lord God made them all.'

I took baby Anne-Marie with me to visit her in Belfast but she never recovered consciousness. I came back to London with a heavy heart.

To help make ends meet, I had some part-time cleaning jobs. As I wouldn't leave the children with anyone, I went out to work at half past five in the morning, and when I got back Paddy would go out to his work. When he came in in the evening, I would go out to my evening job.

The months passed with Mummy making no signs of recovery. I was praying fervently to Our Lady of Perpetual Help, remembering the Thursday novena services I used to attend as a youngster. I believe it is a very powerful prayer and one I made constantly throughout my imprisonment. Before I was married in 1957, I was enrolled in the perpetual novena to Our Lady of Perpetual Help. I still have that enrolment card with its picture of an ancient icon of Mary on it and my name, Annie Smyth as I then was. Throughout my prison sentence, when I felt helpless, I prayed especially to our Lady of Perpetual Help. Jesus is certainly our help and mediator and He is eternal, so as a mother now myself I think it's good to honour and call on the prayers of her who is the mother of our perpetual, eternal help.

I asked Mother Mary that if Mummy was going to survive and be completely helpless and dependent, which she wouldn't have wanted, then to ask Jesus to take her home peacefully to Himself. And if so, to do it on a Thursday so I would know my prayer had been answered.

That Thursday morning, 21 September 1967, I awoke in the middle of the night, around three o'clock, screaming. When Paddy, frightened out of his wits poor thing, asked what was wrong all I could repeat was 'Mummy, Mummy.' He told me it was just that she was too much on my mind. An hour or so later I had to get up to go to my first cleaning job. When I returned and Paddy left for his work, a knock came to our door. It was my good friend and neighbour Leila O'Brien, whom I used to work with in that early-morning job. She had a phone. Her husband had taken a call from Belfast before we came in from work, saying that Mummy had died that Thursday morning.

Mummy was only fifty-four when she died. She had worked so hard all her life to bring us up and to give us the little comforts and extras—like a pair of shoes on our feet. I remember her whitening our plimsolls and washing out our one pair of socks every night, sewing dresses, darning socks. She had so little materially but she left us a richness of legacies in the memory of her goodness and example, as did my dad in his turn.

When I came back after the funeral my two hands and forearms broke out in the most awful rash. It became so painful that I couldn't even bear to put them in water. My friend and neighbour Leila O'Brien actually used to come over to bathe my baby daughter. I went to the doctor and ended up in hospital for a week, my hands and arms swathed in bandages. They diagnosed severe dermatitis and gave me plastic gloves to use when doing all household chores, even making beds and dusting. I still suffer from dermatitis but, thank God, nothing like as badly as I did then. Those plastic gloves were to become infamous some years later.

THREE

People still ask me today where I would rather live—Belfast or London. The truth of the matter is that part of my heart always remained in Northern Ireland. But who could say they would honestly want their children to grow up there today with all that has happened and is still happening? Apart from the tragic 'Troubles,' Belfast is a great place. In some ways I believe Paddy and I would have been better off living over there. For example, we could have bought two decent houses in Belfast for the price of the little house we have in London today. But then, you always come back to the question of the politics, and more so the violence of the Troubles, the troubles which landed on our own doorstep in London.

During my childhood, as I have said, there was no discussion of politics in our home, and only once did I hear of any violence. I think I was about twelve years old when there was a 'shoot-out' in Leesson Street, and one of my friends was on the street at the time. She got caught in the cross-fire and was shot in the leg. I remember someone saying it was the IRA, and that was the only time I ever heard of them when I lived in Belfast. We certainly didn't know who they were, nor ever saw them, and none of my family, uncles, cousins or anybody else, was ever involved.

When the Troubles started in 1969, I worried about my daddy and brothers and sisters. Whenever we heard of a bomb going off near where any of the family lived, we would phone over to make sure they were all right. I still went over with the children in the summer holidays to visit their Grandad. Our family has suffered directly. In 1983, when I was still in prison, Paddy's little eight-year-old nephew was run over by an armoured car and died as a result. The year before we were arrested, my Uncle Bobby, who drove one of my Uncle Vincent Clark's coal lorries, was killed. One day he was called out to a particular hire job and when he arrived Protestant paramilitaries were waiting for him. They tried to hang him and when they failed they shot him dead. It was one of those senseless 'reprisal killings' to avenge the death of a Protestant who had been killed. My Uncle Vincent was assassinated just as brutally and as randomly the next year as he was leaving my Grandmother Clark's home in Whiterock Gardens. He died just because he was a Catholic, as some other man had died just because he was a Protestant. There can hardly be a family or a person in Belfast who doesn't know someone who has been hurt by the Troubles. My sister Mary, for example, worked in the Victoria Infirmary with young Marie Wilson, who was killed in the Enniskillen bombing; this occurred on the morning of Remembrance Sunday, 8 November 1987. As the people of this small Northern Irish town gathered to remember their dead of two World Wars and other conflicts, the town square was devastated by an IRA bomb. Her father Gordon, who was later appointed a Senator in Ireland, went on to become an eloquent spokesman for forgiveness.

We only once witnessed for ourselves the reality of living with the Troubles. I was in Belfast one summer holiday with the children, and taking them to call on Paddy's sister and her husband Giuseppe, parents of Gerard Conlon, later one of the wrongfully-imprisoned 'Guildford Four.' Just as we turned the corner into their street, a whole crowd of soldiers came running towards us, followed by a hail of stones and rocks. Of course my two younger children were terrified and clung on to me, crying. I tried to calm them and said, 'It's all right, it's only some soldiers.' Then a crowd of youths followed, still throwing stones after the army. Then I really began to get frightened, afraid we were going to get caught up in some kind of 'incident.' I ran the next few yards and pulled the children into the Conlons' doorway. Sarah was out, but Giuseppe was there and I told him what we had just witnessed. He shook his head and with a sigh said it was happening around there all the time now, youths goading and stoning the soldiers. Perhaps we were lucky only to witness this one incident, but I can't forget all the people who have to live with the fear of violence all the time. We heard many stories about people suffering abuse from the army and having their homes wrecked in fruitless searches for weapons.

Our last visit before our own troubles began, in the summer of 1974, was to see my sister-in-law Teresa. She told me how there had been some sort of riot in Abyssinia Street. Her little son Michael was playing outside their house when a commotion began. As she pulled him in off the street, a rubber bullet flew past and landed just near her door. If she had not acted just then, it would have hit him. She told me how she picked up the bullet and shouted to the soldiers, 'That's one bullet you won't fire again' and, shaking with nerves, banged her door shut.

When she told me all this I thanked God for little Michael's escape, and asked Teresa what the difference was between a rubber bullet and an ordinary bullet as, thankfully, I had never seen either. She said the Americans were paying £5 for them as some sort of grim souvenir. She handed it to me and I remember thinking how heavy it was. Teresa told me to take it home as a 'souvenir.' I refused her offer but she dropped it into my shopping bag anyway, no doubt thinking it must be valuable if the Americans were paying a fiver for them and that it would be a reminder to us living safely back in London of the hazards faced by them in those troubled times in Belfast. I thought no more of it and it remained at the bottom of that shopping bag. Neither of us could guess at the time the notoriety that that rubber bullet would attain.

When we arrived at the dock we were the last to board the ship after all our goodbyes. One of the dockers shouted to me, 'Come on, Mother, or you'll miss the boat.' As was routine, the police were doing security checks. I was asked to put my bag up on the table for checking. A policeman emptied out the bag. It was full of shoes and a hurley stick for young Patrick and there, sitting among them, was Teresa's rubber bullet. He didn't even mention it, just told me to hurry up or I would miss the boat. It was the only bag he checked.

When we were home and unpacking I showed Paddy the macabre souvenir and told him the story behind it. He told me quite sharply to get it out of sight; he didn't want the children seeing such a sign of violence. I assured him I had no intention of letting them see it and threw it into a drawer of the chest beside which I was unpacking in the back room downstairs. There it remained, untouched and forgotten until the fateful night in December when the police came to our house.

Paddy was unashamedly proud to have been a British soldier, and thought England the best place in the world to live and bring up a family. As others have since pointed out, we had a bust of Winston Churchill, the great wartime leader, in our house. Vincent wanted to be a policeman. The year we were arrested he had started working with the Gas Board, as his father had done before him, and was doing night classes until he was old enough to join. Young Patrick hoped to join the army when he was old enough. After school he would play for hours with his model soldiers. He had collected models of every regiment of the British Army. Their ambitions were not to be realized and their first encounter with the police, the night of 3 December 1974 when they burst into our home, was not to be a happy one. My two sons were to end up in prison for crimes they had not committed.

FOUR

By December 1974 we had been living in our small terraced house at 43 Third Avenue for nearly four years. I had five part-time cleaning jobs at the time. Paddy, for the first time in his life, was out of work, and the atmosphere was a bit tense between us. He must have been depressed about being unemployed since September. I was uptight because I wasn't used to him being around the house in the daytime. I thought he could be doing more to find a job, and resented him drinking and smoking when I felt we couldn't really afford it. I thought it an awful waste of money, although I never begrudged Paddy his pint of an evening. Although he liked a drink, he was never a drunkard nor did he ever mistreat me or his children.

Tuesday 3 December began like any other day. We were completely unaware of the events that were about to unfold. We were beginning the run-up to Christmas and, like any mother, I was buying little bits and pieces each week in preparation. On the Sunday, Paddy had taken out the Christmas tree lights for Anne-Marie, to test that they were in good working order. She was thrilled. Paddy said that rather than put them away in the cupboard again, they could remain in the corner of the sitting room until we put the tree up the following week. They were still there when the police came on the Tuesday night.

We had always tried to make Christmas as special a time as possible for our children. I knew what I was going to buy for Anne-Marie. Patrick was going to get an electric organ from Whiteley's in Queensway.

I had done my first cleaning job in the morning and then left Anne-Marie at her school, which was only two blocks away from us. On my return the telephone rang. It was our old friend Pat O'Neil. His wife Helen had gone into hospital to have another baby, and he asked if I could look after their three little girls. I said that would be fine, feeling sure I could get the two older girls into Anne-Marie's school for the few days they would be with us as I was quite friendly with the headmistress. The youngest girl I would take along with me to my cleaning jobs. So we agreed that Pat would drop off the girls that evening.

I told Paddy about the phone call from Pat and headed out to my next job. It must have been around ten o'clock. On Tuesdays I used to wash out two shops—one mens-wear and the other ladies-wear. I finished about half past twelve and popped into the supermarket on the Harrow Road to do some shopping. On the way home I called in at another shop which I cleaned, because I knew there was a jumble sale on that day in the premises next door. I left my shopping with Rita the shopowner, and her assistant Marie, and I went to the jumble sale.

My brother Sean was staying with us and working on a building site where, not surprisingly, he quickly wore out jumpers and shirts. So that day at the jumble sale I got a few shirts for him. I also bought some accessories for my vacuum cleaner. It was an upright model and I needed the pieces which allowed you to clean upholstery.

We went back into the shop and had a cup of tea before I picked up my shopping to head home. The owner's young son came in and offered to help me home with my shopping. As I didn't buy two or three pounds of potatoes at a time, but rather at least a ten-pound bag, his help was all the more appreciated. When we arrived home on foot he said, 'Cor blimey, Mrs Maguire, what have you got in here, a bleedin' bomb or something?' I told him to 'Get on out of it' and he laughed as he headed off. Later that night as I recounted my movements of the day in every detail, I told the police that. Of course, they said to me, 'Well, was it a bomb?'

When I came into the house I shouted, 'Hello, who's in?' and popped my head around the sitting-room door. John and his girlfriend Maxine were there along with John's mate Hugh McHugh who was known as Ginger. Our children's friends were always welcome in the house—I was happy that they felt they could bring them in and it meant that I knew where they were. I always gave the visitors exactly the same as I was giving my own children. On this occasion it was burgers in buns.

As I carried them in to the sitting-room, I noticed a suitcase behind the settee and asked whose it was. None of them knew. The previous year Paddy had been in hospital to get help for a drink problem. Many people suffer from this problem and most try to keep it hidden. Paddy's not like that. He is a very open and straightforward person and says what he thinks. My first reaction when I saw this suitcase was that it belonged to someone he had met in that clinic and had told to look him up if ever he needed help. Neither of us would ever see anyone out on the street, if we could put them up for a while, on the understanding that it was only until they got sorted out.

I was the same with my neighbours. I was not one for having people sitting around my house, but I tried to let them know that I was always there if anyone needed help. They were welcome to use our phone. I would lend someone a few pounds rather than see them, or especially their children, go short. The only neighbour I saw regularly was Teresa Roache who often popped in for a coffee. You couldn't help but like Teresa. Even the children loved it when she came in. She was a Dubliner and a very funny person. Even if you had been feeling down, you would be laughing by the time Teresa left the house.

With relations between Paddy and me being tense, and with the strain of trying to make ends meet, prepare for Christmas and buy the children's presents, I was in no mood to have an extra person in our house. I even said to John, 'If he thinks there's another drinker coming in he's mistaken.'

I sat down with the young folks a moment before they went out. Vincent was back from his job at the Gas Board and was in his room preparing for his night class at college.

Two parcels came from the mail order catalogue I ran. One was for Teresa Roache containing roller skates and games for her children's Christmas, and the other was for another neighbour. When my son Patrick came in from school, I sent him out twice to deliver these parcels.

I prepared a pot of stew for the evening's dinner and, as it was cooking, did some housework. Even though I had my five jobs and my children to look after, I was still terribly houseproud and would dust and clean different rooms on different days, always being careful to put on my plastic gloves first as I had been told, to avoid needless irritation of the dermatitis on my hands. Then Teresa Roache called in, so we sat down and had a cup of coffee and a blether [a chat] together.

When Teresa left, I began to wash the kitchen floor. I had just started when the front door opened and into the kitchen came Paddy with Giuseppe Conlon, his brother-in-law from Belfast. My first reaction was, 'Good Lord, what are you doing here, Giuseppe?' I knew that he was not a well man, having suffered for years from TB. He did look ill and was gasping for breath. The journey from Belfast must have taken a lot out of him. I told them to go into the sitting-room and made a cup of tea.

While I had been at work, Paddy had received a telegram from the Conlons' solicitor saying that Giuseppe was on his way to London as his son Gerard had been arrested. It wasn't the first time that Giuseppe had had to bail his son out from trouble. As Gerard has himself admitted, he was, at the time, a small-time criminal and petty thief.

When I sat down with them, Giuseppe told me that Gerard had been arrested on suspicion of the Guildford bombing, where two pubs had been bombed, five innocent people killed and many injured. I cried out, 'O God, not that, Giuseppe. Jesus, no, not that.'

It would have been bad enough when strangers do something like that, but the thought that it could have been one of your own was too much to bear, too evil to contemplate. Gerard Conlon was my nephew, the son of Paddy's sister. He was a silly young man who had caused his parents enough grief with his petty thieving. Even when we took him in once to help him out for the sake of his parents, he stole from the children's piggy banks to feed his drug habit. But we still considered him our nephew and Giuseppe was adamant that his son was not involved in terrorism. I told him that he knew his own son just as I knew mine, and I hoped to God for his sake that he was right.

Giuseppe had called Paddy's brother Hugh and his wife Kitty, but there was no reply. They had been sent a telegram as well.

Poor Giuseppe sat in the armchair. I could see he was absolutely exhausted and suggested he have a nap for an hour while we continued to phone Hugh and Kitty. I told him that they had perhaps gone away for the weekend, but if they had come back he could go and stay with them. Equally, he was just as welcome to stay with us.

At around five o'clock the dinner was ready. Giuseppe was so upset, he could only eat a very little. He phoned his wife Sarah in Belfast and I had a word with her too, assuring her we would do whatever we could to help Giuseppe. She too was adamant that her son Gerard was not involved in any way with the IRA or terrorism.

There was still no answer from Hugh and Kitty so we left a message with the wife of a good friend of theirs and ours, Sean Tully. Later he called and said he would come over and see us. On the way, he called at Hugh and Kitty's house. The woman in the flat downstairs told him that the police had taken them away on the Saturday morning. They had been in custody all weekend and none of us knew.

Before Sean arrived, Paddy had gone out to the local police station on the Harrow Road without telling us. He explained that there was no reply from his brother's house. He was worried that something might have happened to them. Paddy had worked with the Gas Board for many years and I think he feared that they might have been gassed or poisoned from a faulty appliance. He asked the police if they could go with him to his brother's house and break down the door if necessary. The police must have known that Hugh and Kitty were being held in custody, but they certainly didn't say so to Paddy. We later learned that Hugh and Kitty had been arrested because Gerard Conlon had once stayed with them. Their house was ransacked and they were kept in custody for a week, finally being released without charge. They are another innocent family who went through hell. Always hard-working people, their lives were destroyed by what happened. Kitty's nerves were shattered and she has never recovered.

Although that same day my name was being given to the police by Paul Hill and Gerard Conlon, I believe the police decided to come to our house when Paddy visited the police station about his brother and sister-in-law. At the trial they claimed that they had been observing our house for a couple of days. We still don't believe that. The people in that area knew the police and certainly noticed strangers. The police said they had kept watch on our house from a block of flats opposite. When I was out on bail awaiting trial, I decided to make my own enquiries. All the tenants on that block swore that no police had been in any of their flats or in the building. If the police had been keeping watch on our house, why didn't they stop Patrick either of the times he went out of our house carrying parcels, once through the very flats opposite, the other time around the corner to a house near the dairy? If, as they claimed, we were manufacturing explosives, surely they would have seen in that an opportunity to catch us 'red-handed'?

When I think back on it, there were several other occasions that day when, if the police really believed we were dealing with explosives, they could have intervened. Pat O'Neil arrived at our house in the evening with his three little girls and he was carrying a holdall with their clothes in it. Then Sean Tully arrived in his car to tell us of Hugh and Kitty's arrest.

Between six and half past six in the evening, my brother Sean came in from work, having gone out before six in the morning. He was working as many hours as he could because he was going home to Belfast at Christmas. Sean, of course, was horrified like all of us at the news. But his next reaction baffled me a bit. He said, 'You know, love, they'll be coming here next.' That, apparently, was the routine in Northern Ireland. When someone was arrested on suspicion of terrorism, the rest of the family was visited by the police and questioned. If they did come, I thought, we had nothing to worry about.

Sean had his dinner. Pat didn't want any and his girls said they didn't like stew. Vincent had left for his night class, but early, to catch the shops, as he wanted to buy a new pair of shoes on the way. Patrick and John went out to their youth club at the bottom of Third Avenue. As the girls didn't want stew, I said I would make them egg and chips. So I took Anne-Marie and Pat's girl Jacqueline, who was about the same age, around to the fish and chip shop. It was pouring with rain and we went out with a bag to carry the chips in, and umbrellas. (Another person going out of our house with a bag!) I always liked to be jolly with children and, as it was bucketing down, we started singing 'I'm singing in the rain' as we walked down the avenue. At the bottom, we met John and Patrick with their friends. They were soaked because the church hall wasn't open yet. I went to the side door where the hallkeeper was and told him the youngsters were waiting to get in. He opened the hall doors right away.

When we arrived at the fish and chip shop Anne-Marie found a fifty-pence piece on the floor and told the shopowner. That is how we had brought them up. If you find anything, you hand it over. To her delight, the shopowner told her to keep it. Right away she said she would share it with Jacqueline.

We bought our chips and headed home, where I fried eggs and the children sat down to eat. I tried to persuade Pat O'Neil to have something before he left and he eventually agreed to eat just a 'chip buttie.' (That chip buttie was later to raise a laugh in court when I recounted everything we had done that day, and at that point the judge decided we had better recess for lunch or we would be lucky even to get a chip buttie!)

My husband Paddy invited Pat to go over to the local pub for a drink before leaving, but Pat's wife Helen always watched a TV programme that evening, and he said she was going to telephone him at our house when it was finished. So they all watched the programme as well. When Helen phoned, Paddy spoke to her as well. I remember his joking about their baby number four. He said they were heading towards a football team.

Before the men went to the pub, I said I would use the peace and quiet to do my washing. I told Anne-Marie to take out her crayons and colouring books for the girls to play with and said that if they were good I would take them swimming after school the next day.

I pulled out my washing machine, a then quite modern twin-tub. The younger generation laugh when they see such contraptions today! I sorted the clothes into different piles on the floor according to colour. John came in from the youth club. I was filling the washing machine when the doorbell rang, immediately followed by a banging on the door.

CHAPTER
FIVE

I looked through the window in the kitchen door, thinking it was the men already back from the pub. Either that or Pat had decided not to go after all and the others had returned.

As the bell had rung, Anne-Marie had run to answer it. That was almost twenty years ago, but my daughter can still recount exactly how that door came flying in. It was lucky she hadn't quite reached it or she would have been knocked over and injured. She can still repeat the words, in the exact accent, of the first policeman (I later learned his name was Mundy) who stormed in and asked if her mum was at home. At the time Anne-Marie was eight years old.

The policemen were all in plain clothes, except for the officers with sniffer dogs who followed them. Mundy asked me if I was Annie Maguire. (Gerard Conlon and family and friends in Belfast call me 'Annie'.) When I said I was, he asked me to switch off my washing machine and come through to the sitting-room. Anne-Marie was screaming, in shock from the door being banged in and from fear of the big dogs. She ran over and clung on to me. I was afraid of the dogs myself, having been bitten by an Alsatian as a child. I asked the men who they were and what they wanted, and Mundy told me again to get into the sitting-room. He ordered the others to take the dogs upstairs.

I tried to calm Anne-Marie and the O'Neil girls who were all crying, and told them to go back to their colouring books while I had a talk with the policemen.

I had cross-over net curtains on my sitting-room window and heavy side curtains which were never closed, just as my door was never locked. That was the way we lived in the Avenues in those days. All the children were in and out of my house. Since the curtains were still ajar, therefore, and if, as they claimed, they had been watching us, they would have seen who was in earlier and who went out.

By this time, our house was like a police station. I remembered what my brother Sean had said. I asked if they were there because of Gerard Conlon. They said they were, and asked me what I knew about him. I said, 'Very little, but his father is here.' The policeman appeared surprised, which still makes me question their statement later under oath that Giuseppe had been followed from the boat. I told them Giuseppe had come over and was to see a solicitor the next morning for his son. Mundy asked me who else lived in the house. I told him about my brother Sean, and how he was going home for Christmas. I also told him that the little O'Neil girls were there while their mummy was in hospital. I found it strange that he persisted in asking me who else lived there, but I spelled out that it was my husband and four children.

He asked where the men were at the moment. I was surprised. I said they couldn't have missed them surely, as they had just gone out. It couldn't have been more than four or five minutes before. Again, this casts doubt on the later police claim that they had been watching our house: if they had, they would have seen the men going out. The front door was the only exit.

From my sitting-room window you could see the sign of The Lancers' pub where the men had gone. You had to go down past some flats to reach it. I pointed out the sign to Mundy. He told me he had not seen anyone leave the front door. I estimated that they must have only been halfway to the pub when the police came round the corner onto our avenue. At the trial, the police made out that the men had gone over the wall from our back garden into Ilbert Street to dispose of explosives. Despite their claims that we had possessed explosives in our house, they never found any, either there or in the whole surrounding area which they searched later that night.

Some policemen told fifteen-year-old John to go with them to point out his father and the other men. Yet again, I feel this gave the lie to their claim that they had been watching us; they would have known what the men looked like. As they were leaving our house my sixteen-year-old, Vincent, came in from his night class.

At the pub Paddy turned round and saw John with the policemen. He asked what was wrong, and did he want him? Again, if he or the other men had been involved in criminal activity, I don't think he would so readily have identified himself. The police asked the men to come outside. Pat O'Neil later joked that The Lancers' owed them a round of drinks, as they had just bought one and never had time to drink it!

Back in the house, the police started asking me questions about Gerard Conlon. I told them I did not know anything about him or indeed about any other nephew or niece living back in Belfast. They lived over there, we lived over here. I told him that I knew more about the youngsters who lived around us on the Avenue. Mundy asked me if I had anyone who could look after the children. When I asked why, he replied that they needed to ask me some more questions. Naively, I said he could do it right there in the house. He insisted I would have to go to the police station—along with my three sons. When he mentioned my three sons I snapped and became hysterical. I told him to leave them alone, that they were English born and bred.

When he asked me again if I knew someone who could look after the children, the first name which came to mind was that of Teresa Roache. Anne-Marie loved her so, and I knew the girls would be all right with Teresa. The police sent across for her.

A couple of policemen came back with John. The men were being taken to Paddington Green police station. Mundy let me prepare the girls for bed. I tried to reassure them that I would be back soon, saying that the boys and I were just going to see if we could help the policemen and policeladies. Poor little Anne-Marie's lips were trembling as she fought back the tears. I put them into our bed, the two little ones in the middle and Jacqueline and Anne-Marie on the outside, telling them they were the big girls and they should look after the little ones. I said Teresa would be across soon to look after them. I did not know then that the policewoman was going to stay too. I kissed the three little O'Neil girls goodnight. When I kissed Anne-Marie she just clung to me. It was as if my little eight-year-old daughter knew what I then did not: that I would not be back soon.

The policewoman had come with me to the bedroom. I had recently re-decorated it with matching curtains and bed linen from Marks and Spencer's, the national chain of food and clothes stores. As I was dressing the children for bed she was saying how expensive it must have been to have all this matching linen. I told her about my jobs, and that if you got little things week by week, spread out the cost, that was how you could manage these things.

She started looking in drawers and cupboards. I used to buy damaged cans from a neighbour who worked in a food factory. My mother had always had food in the cupboard and that was my first priority too. In one cupboard there was a box of tins of baked beans with no labels. The policewoman remarked that I had plenty of food in and I said, 'Yes, for the boys.' I meant, of course, for my sons, the boys, as often when they came in from school with their friends they would have beans or spaghetti on toast. We always sat down for a proper meal together when Paddy came in from work. But the police were to put a different interpretation on my use of the term 'the boys.'

I put my coat on—it was leather with a fur trim, fashionable at the time—and took my handbag. Later, I was to realize that I had forgotten my glasses. I did have my purse in the bag which was fairly heavy because that day I had emptied Patrick's piggy bank to put into his post office account the next day. Remember, Patrick was only thirteen at the time.

I went downstairs with the officer. My three sons were standing at the bottom surrounded by policemen. At that moment I thought to myself, 'My God, do you deserve this?'

We were an ordinary family getting on with life as best we could. All our little problems were soon to pale into insignificance.

SIX

They took me away in a police car and the three boys in a van, a 'meat wagon' I believe they call it. Despite my earlier fears I was honestly not worried. As I had never had any dealings with the police, I thought all this must be a normal procedure. I thought their late entrance must be the normal routine when a member of a family was arrested. I assumed we would be at the police station for half an hour or an hour, and then I could get back to my daughter and the little O'Neil girls.

When we arrived at Harrow Road police station, I was taken into one room and the boys off somewhere else. They started doing swabs; wiping my hands with cotton wool which had been dipped in some sort of liquid. As the person doing it took my hand to begin, he commented on my nails being so short and I told him I had always bitten them. He remarked also on the roughness of my hands and I said that it was down to hard work. I smarted when he applied a liquid with cotton wool, as my hands were cracked. When he looked up in surprise, I told him I had dermatitis. He did fingernail scrapes and took my fingerprints and then started asking me more questions. I told him that I didn't have answers to all these questions; that I had already told them I knew nothing about Gerard Conlon.

It must have been around midnight when they took me back out to the hallway where my three boys were already sitting. I told them we would be going home now, that they were finished with us. I did think that the procedure we had gone through was rather excessive, but still I wasn't worried. I still trusted the police and had confidence in them. I just told myself it was their job.

I thought they were about to take us home when Mundy walked in. He was carrying a little bundle in his hands. 'Who owns these wigs?' he said. I told him they were mine. He asked who owned the plastic disposable gloves? I said I did. He asked what I used them for and I told him about my skin complaint. 'Dermatitis,' I said, 'but also for other things.' Immediately he snapped back, 'What other things?' I told him I wore them when cleaning brass—I had lots of brass ornaments which I liked to keep shining clean—and I also wore them when in the garden. It had even reached the stage that I had to use them when dusting. He seemed to be very interested in these plastic gloves; he didn't have them with him but obviously had seen them in my kitchen drawer. He asked when I had last used them, and that's when I told him about the bundle I had just put out with the rubbish that evening. I said that he could go and check for himself, even telling him that there were two dustbins outside the house and the gloves were near the top of the one which was full up. I told him I had just cleared out a kitchen drawer that day and that there was also a pair of woollen gloves with the fingers cut off. Young Patrick had these old woollen gloves for football. They were full of holes and if I had thrown them out once, I had thrown them out a dozen times! Yet he always retrieved them.

The wigs were significant, I was to learn later, as they were after a blonde-haired woman for the Guildford bombings. One of my wigs unfortunately happened to be what they called a 'dirty blonde.' Wigs were quite fashionable at the time. The previous year, a girlfriend of one of Paddy's friends had given me one, but I never wore it. What would I be wanting to change my hair colour for? It was not as if I went to fancy parties or cocktail parties or anything like that. Very occasionally Paddy and I would pop round to the local bar, and at the weekend Paddy would go to the British Legion Club or the local Conservative Club. Not the sort of places I would be putting wigs on to go to! The other wig I acquired just before Anne-Marie's birthday in October. I was walking around Brixton Market with Helen O'Neil (who was in hospital the night we were arrested) to buy a doll's pram, and we saw this stall full of them. Always ready for a laugh, Helen goaded me, 'Come on, Maguire, try one of these on.' We had such a laugh that I said I would take it and play a joke on Paddy when he came in from work. When he saw me he cried out, 'In the name of God, what have you done with your hair?' When I told him it was a wig we had such a laugh. That was the only time I ever wore it. Afterwards, Anne-Marie and her friends used them for playing and dressing up.

The wigs and the gloves, including Patrick's holey woollen ones, were to be produced in court as 'evidence' that we were running a 'bomb-making factory' in our little house on Third Avenue. But that night in the police station, I didn't make any connection. All that was going through my mind was how late it was and that I wanted to get home to Anne-Marie and the O'Neil girls, and get my boys home for school and work the next morning.

A policeman came over to us and told the boys he would take them home so, quite naturally, I stood up to go with them. 'No, not you,' he said. Thirteen-year-old

Patrick said he didn't want to leave without his mum and sat down again. The police officer told him not to give them 'any hassle.' I told Patrick and the other boys just to go, that Anne-Marie needed them, that their coming home would reassure her and that I would be home soon. That is what I honestly thought. I had no reason to think otherwise.

So the three lads left with the policeman and I was left sitting on the bench. Some other officers came over to me and one said, 'Right, down here.' I got up and followed them. I didn't even realize that they were taking me to the cells. As we entered the corridor, I saw smoke pouring out of a room and cried out, 'O God, something's on fire.' The man in front shouted to the others to get me out of there quick. And they did. They literally ran me out, my feet hardly touching the ground!

I learned much later that Carole Richardson and her friend Lisa Astin, who had been arrested on suspicion of the Guildford bombing, were in two of the cells. Someone had given Lisa a light for a cigarette and she had set fire to the mattress in the cell. The scene appears quite funny today but it certainly wasn't at the time.

Once the mattress fire was out, I was brought back down to the cells and incarcerated until the next morning. Needless to say, I didn't sleep a wink that night and saw in the dawn. By now I was asking myself what on earth I was doing there. Was it just because I was Gerard Conlon's aunt? I was praying, asking God to give me strength, asking what was happening to me. I should have been at home with my husband and children, and I was abandoned in a cell in Harrow Road police station.

Next morning, someone came to my cell and asked if anyone could look after the children. I asked what he meant; I was going home and could look after my children myself. 'No,' he said, 'you're going to Guildford.' He told me it was for more questioning. I stressed again that I couldn't answer any more questions; I didn't know anything about the things they were asking me. I could please myself, he said. Either I knew someone who could look after Patrick and Anne-Marie, the younger two, or they would put them 'into care.' I could scarcely take this in. Paddy and I were parents who loved our children and would hardly let them out of our sight, and someone was talking of putting them into a home. The first name that came to my mind was that of my Aunt Teasy, who lived with her husband Bill in Kennington.

They took me to Guildford in the back of a police car. As a wife and mother I would often be shopping on the Edgware Road, popping into Marks and Spencer's, or taking my child to school in the morning. When we saw police vans going up and down Harrow Road taking prisoners to the courts the children would get excited. Now, this morning of 4 December 1974, it was I speeding down the road in the company of the police. I should have been taking my child to school. As the car turned round by Marks and Spencer's I saw a neighbour with her children and then began to cry.

One of the officers said that the route must be familiar to me. I said I had never been to Guildford before. 'Oh no?' he replied. I told him I did not even know where it was. Neither Paddy or I had even known there was a Guildford in England before seeing the news reports of the terrible bombings there. We had only ever heard of Guilford in Northern Ireland. By this stage I think I was in a state of shock.

The officers kept saying that I no doubt recognized this or that building or road or landmark. There were people gathered outside Guildford police station when we arrived, and the young policeman sitting with me in the back gave me a coat and told me to put it over my head. I said that I'd done nothing wrong and had no need to cover my head. It was the sort of thing one reads about and it was happening to me. In front, I saw a police van and could make out Paddy and Sean waving through the back window. Nearer the station, I could hear the crowd shouting, 'Hang the Irish bastards, hang them.' It was a horrible nightmare.

I remember there was a desk at the entrance. The young policeman who had been sitting beside me in the car asked if I would like a drink of water. Just at that moment a door opened and two men appeared—I found out later that their names were Powell and Robinson. The one named Robinson shouted, 'Get her in here.' I was taken into an interrogation room. There we sat and they asked me more and more questions. Was I Anne Maguire and did I know why I was there? To this I answered yes, that I was there to answer questions about Gerard Conlon. What did I know about him? I told them that just as I had told the other policeman the night before, I only knew that his father, Giuseppe, had arrived at our house the day before and that I believed him when he said Gerard was not involved with the IRA. He asked me what I would say if he told me that Gerard Conlon had 'implicated me,' had made a statement saying I showed him how to make bombs? Of course, I just could not believe it. At this stage they didn't mention Paul Hill, or any of the others they had arrested, only Gerard Conlon. I told them that if Gerard had said that, he was telling lies, that he knew his Uncle Paddy had been in the British Army and was what some people classed as 'pro-British.' No way did we involve ourselves in politics and certainly not terrorism. I had expressed my hope to many people that those dastardly bombers would be caught. At that, they started mocking me. 'Oh yeah, sure, she wants the bombers caught, it's nothing to do with her of course.' They continued asking questions. Again, they took my fingerprints. One man kept coming in and saying things like my husband had told them that I didn't have five cleaning jobs, that I was prostituting, that he refused to sleep with me and so on. This was just so ridiculous that I asked them to bring Paddy into the room and say the same thing in person. Of course, they didn't. They said that Gerard told them I had gone to Guildford with these other people and planted bombs. I replied 'No sir, he is telling lies.' I always called the police officers 'sir' as I had been brought up to do. Then they brought in an older man. I told them I didn't know him. He was in a terrible state, obviously badly beaten. They took him away and then brought in Paul Hill. When I say 'brought in,' I mean dragged in. They practically had to carry him and then hold him up, as he couldn't stand. I don't think he could even have spoken, his face was in such a mess. His eyes were swollen up like balloons, and I don't even know if he could see me. He didn't say anything, just stared, eyes glazed, straight ahead. I had seen him once before but, because of the state he was in, I only recognized him by the jacket he was wearing, the same one as he had had on before. I said that it was Paul Hill. At that, they turned him around and dragged him out again.

They said that he had told them I taught him how to make bombs in my kitchen. I replied that if Paul Hill had ever been in my kitchen, they should ask him to describe it, because I knew that he had never been in my house. Gerard Conlon had been in my house, but about two years before.

The reason I recognized Paul Hill and his sports jacket was that, some weeks previously, I had gone to a dance in a social centre at Camden. It was the one and only time I had been to an Irish dance in London, and I was quite surprised to find that most of the people there were English. I suppose they liked the music; there was an Irish band playing. The only reason I went was because Paddy's brother, Hugh, had bought the ticket for me, saying a night out would do us good. I didn't want to let him down by not going. It was only the week after the Guildford bombings, and at one point an English couple sitting beside us spoke about that terrible event. I remember very clearly that I joined in the expressions of revulsion and said that if the bombers thought they could start doing over here what they were doing in Belfast they had better think again; the British people and authorities would not stand for it and they would soon catch them and deal with them. We were all being urged to be security-conscious. On the way in to the dance, there were two men on the door. As we walked in, I said to one of them, 'Well, fine security men you make, I could have anything in this bag.' They just laughed, but I was not joking. I believed that if there were to be security checks, then they should be for everybody and should be done conscientiously.

Gerard Conlon was there with a group of his friends from the hostel they were staying in on Kilburn's Quex Road. (Kilburn is an area of North London often referred to as 'Little Ireland' because of the large number of Irish people who have settled there.) Relations were not very good between Gerard and me and my children since our earlier experience. I forgave him, as I forgive him today for what he did to us, but I couldn't forget and I preferred not to have any dealings with him. I even asked Hugh to keep him away from me as I was still angry at what he had done and didn't want any unpleasantness. A couple of the young lads sat down near us at one point and we made conversation. One was Danny Wilson from Belfast. It turned out I had known his mother when we worked in the weaving together. The other lad said maybe I knew his mother as well. When he told me his mother's maiden name and where her family had lived, I said of course, I knew her. We were at the 'wee Leessie' together. That was all I had said to Paul Hill until I saw him dragged in before me at Guildford police station. When I told the police this they said it had been an IRA dance to 'celebrate' the Guildford bombing.

Next they brought in Gerard Conlon. To this day, Gerard's recollection of that event and mine are different. He was not in as bad a state as Paul Hill. At least he was able to walk in. I asked him, 'Did you write that statement son?' He said to the police, 'You've got what you want.' I told him, 'Gerard, you know this is lies. Why don't you tell the truth?' Then he looked at me and said, 'You tell the truth,' and they led him away. I forgive Gerard and Paul, but I cannot forget what they brought upon our family and other families. Why did they give my name and not the name of their own mothers or sisters or girlfriends? They have yet to tell me why, or to apologize.

The interrogation went on and on. I don't know how long I was there. I am told now it was nearly a week. But I lost track of time. Day merged into night. I was in a state of shock and disorientation, compounded by a lack of sleep, food and fluid. Because I didn't have my glasses with me and also through lack of sleep, my eyes were sore. I was not going to sleep, but every so often I would close my eyes in an effort to rest them. One of the police would come up behind me and push me, saying things like 'You're the bomber, aren't you, you Irish bastard?' I kept saying in return, 'No, sir, I'm not. You've made a mistake.' They made fun of this, saying, 'Listen to her. They've got her well trained with her "yes, sir, no, sir, three bags full, sir".'

I can never forget the beatings and the way they humiliated me. When I was sitting in the chair, they would keep hitting me around the head and ears from behind. As they had seen me rubbing my eyes and trying to rest them, they would pull my head back by the hair and shine this light into my eyes, saying they knew I was the murdering Irish bastard and had better give them the information they wanted. At one stage—it seems quite pathetic now when I think of it—they left a tap dripping. I was sitting behind this table, one of them was sitting opposite watching me and another was further back against the opposite wall. After a while I said, 'Excuse me, sir, but I think someone has left the tap running slightly.' He was furious and pushed my head, telling me not to be smart. I lost track of day and night, date and time. Occasionally I would be thrown into a cell with no mattress or blanket and try to get some sleep. But the light was constantly on, and every few minutes someone would bang on the door to keep me awake. Then I would be taken out again for more interrogation. By this stage, I stank too.

They had taken my shoes and tights away, and would make me stand spreadeagled against a wall, arms and legs outstretched. I was weak and had a very heavy period. I kept falling down. They would just kick and kick me, using foul and abusive language, telling me to get up. Their kicks struck around the lower back and kidney area. I would somehow manage to get up, but not for long. Soon I would collapse again and they would grab me by the hair, pulling and kicking me around the room. When I arrived in Brixton after being charged later the same week and was seen by a doctor, they noticed huge clumps of my hair were missing. My kidneys have never been right since, on account of the kicking and the lack of fluids during that week.

At one stage during the interrogation, an officer held a gun against my head and kept clicking it as he told me I had better tell them what they wanted to hear. I repeated that we had done nothing wrong and were not involved with the IRA or any sort of terrorism. I said I was not afraid to meet my Maker as I had done nothing wrong and was telling the truth. He said I might meet my Maker soon enough if he lost his temper with this gun. They kept telling me I would be going away for a long, long time, that I had murdered a young girl at Guildford.

Yet, despite all the beatings and humiliations, there was one thing that hurt me more than anything. At the time they were taking yet another set of fingerprints. My nerves must have been shattered. I couldn't keep my hands from shaking and in the end they gave up, saying, 'Take the Irish bastard away, we're charging her with murder anyway.' Here was I, a working wife and mother who loved children, being charged with killing some mother's child. I kept fainting and coming round again, going from faint to consciousness. I wanted to wake up and realize it was all a nasty dream. But it wasn't.

SEVEN

I'm told I was detained at Guildford for almost a week—which would have been possible under the then newly-enacted Prevention of Terrorism Act. But for me reality had disappeared. I do remember, though, being transferred from Guildford to Godalming where they were officially to charge me.

I was in the back of a small police car with a blanket over my head, handcuffed to a policewoman they called Babs. I was feeling faint from the heat and claustrophobia, but when I tried to lift it away from my face Babs pulled it down and told me to leave it alone. A male officer was driving, and beside him in front sat an older policewoman called Nancy. This was the second week in December and they were talking about Christmas approaching. Babs said I wouldn't see Christmas at home this year, or for many years to come, and that my children would not have a happy Christmas either. I asked what she meant about my children and asked where they were. She told me they were going to find the worst foster parents in England for them. I cried out that the children had done nothing wrong. No, but I had, she taunted—and my children would suffer for it. I repeated that I had done nothing wrong either. She went on and on about how Anne-Marie and Patrick would be abused and would have no more happy Christmases.

When we arrived at Godalming they couldn't remove the handcuffs as my arm was swollen from being continually pulled and jerked during the journey. Throughout the whole hellish experience, when I was reviled, called the lowest of the low and felt totally abandoned, there were certain human beings who displayed a bit of decent humanity. I have not, and never will, forget those individuals. One such was the sergeant on reception duty at that station. He told another officer to fetch a wet cloth to put over my arm to reduce the swelling. The policewoman pulled at my arm again and said she would soon get the thing off. The sergeant rebuked her and told her I was his prisoner now, in his care. Once he had removed the cuffs he said to her, 'I would advise you to leave now.' He then took me over to a seat and sat me down, proffering me a cup of hot tea. After all I had been through, I could not even relate to this simple act of human kindness and just looked at him warily. He must have sensed my fear and said, 'Look, love, just drink it. I'm a family man myself.' I blurted out, 'Sir, I haven't done anything. Why are they doing this to me and my family?' He said I would have my day and my say.

I was taken into a room where there was a senior police officer, another man writing things in a book, two policemen and the kindly sergeant. The officer who had the air of being a very senior person in the force held a book in his hand. I was held up by two female officers as I could barely stand. I'd had no sleep since being arrested, nor anything to eat, and very little to drink. We faced the senior officer who started reading out of his book, 'I charge you, Anne Rita Maguire, with the murder of Carol...' I didn't even hear the second name. I know

now it was the young girl killed in the pub bombing at Guildford. As he read the charge I just screamed out, 'No, no, no.' I was not guilty, I hadn't murdered anybody, I hated terrorists as much as they did.

I must have passed out, for the next thing I knew I was coming round in a cell with a policewoman and the sergeant putting a blanket around me. I was shaking like a leaf and he told someone to go and get another blanket for me. That man must have been on duty all night, as he kept coming to my cell and asking if I was all right. I could hear myself faintly saying, 'I am not guilty. I am not guilty.'

The next morning when daylight appeared, he came and asked me if I would like to come out of the cell and have a wash. I have to say I stank like a pig. I hope I never again have to live in such a state. I had nothing to wash with as everything had been taken from me when I was arrested. A young policewoman said I had money in my purse (remember I had emptied Patrick's piggy bank) and if I wanted to take some out of it, she would go and buy me what I needed. She counted out some money in front of me and bought me clean underwear, talcum powder and other toiletries.

While I was getting washed for the first time since my arrest—hardly a proper wash, at the sink outside the cells—my Aunt Teasy and Aunt Lizzie arrived at the station with some clean clothes. Aunt Lizzie, who has since died, used to say every time she saw me afterwards that she would never forget the sight of me that day. I was like something that had been dragged through a hedge backwards. I had about ten minutes with my aunts, and then must have fallen asleep again, I was so weak with it all. Then I was being told that my solicitor was there to see me, a young woman by the name of Jenny Sterring. I waited for her in a room with the two officers who had interrogated me most of the time, Powell and Robinson. Powell said that if they didn't get me on the murder charge, they would get me on the gloves, and in either case I would be going down for a very long time. I pleaded with him again to believe my innocence.

Jenny the solicitor had brought young Patrick along with her to see his mum. Seeing the state I was in after a week of interrogation and mistreatment must have had a most disturbing effect on my thirteen-year-old son. In fact, I think it did mark him, along with everything else he was to go through in the months and years ahead. When he came into the room with Jenny, he just looked at me and froze. Then he launched himself at Officer Powell. Poor little kid—he no doubt decided that nobody was going to treat his mum like that. The officers grabbed him and told him to behave himself or he would be put out. Jenny tried to calm him down. I told her what they had said to me just before she came in. She asked Powell if it was true. He never answered her, just smirked. They were present the whole time I was supposed to be having a consultation with my solicitor. I hadn't seen a legal representative at all during the interrogation, before I was charged. Now my interrogators were standing over us as we tried to talk.

Some people say there should be an independent person there when you are being questioned, something like the French system of a 'juge d'instruction,' an 'investigating magistrate' separate from the police. I too am firmly of that opinion. Perhaps some people would play on it, but I believe it might help people who were in our situation. Even if it only helped eliminate the beatings in police stations, it would be worth it. The Guildford Four, beaten into submission, signed false 'confessions.'

I can't blame them for that and anyway they retracted them in court, claiming they had been beaten.

None of us, 'The Maguire Seven' as we became known, signed or gave any false confessions. We maintained our innocence all along, from day one. What do the police hope to gain from all this violence? They may obtain false confessions but in the end—one year, ten years, twenty years—the truth will out and an innocent person will be proved as such. Today, after all the violence they inflicted on us and others in similar situations, they have achieved nothing. They have only left scars on innocent people and discredited the police force. And they have to live with that for the rest of their lives, as well as knowing that they still have not caught the real perpetrators of the crimes. To my mind, when the police treat suspects or prisoners as they treated us, they are putting themselves on the same level as the men of violence in the IRA or UDA. Why did they beat up a thirteen-year-old like my Patrick—surely the only child detained, beaten up and imprisoned under The Prevention of Terrorism Act in mainland Britain? I will never understand it.

The day after being charged with murder, I was to be taken to Brixton prison. I suppose I must have appeared in court but I honestly do not remember. Since the police officer had read out the charge in the police station, I was in a deeper state of shock and seemed to be living in a haze, going in and out of semi-consciousness. As I was being taken to Brixton I do remember passing another cell, the door of which was open. There appeared to be an old woman lying all crumpled up on the floor. I asked the policeman accompanying me if she was all right. He looked at me in disbelief and told me it was not an old woman. Didn't I know her? I soon found out that the 'old lady' was Carole Richardson. The police really believed we knew each other, that we were both part of the same IRA bombing team.

Later, when I was taken out to a police van to be transferred to the prison, I found another girl already sitting in the back. Each of us was accompanied by two officers. As we were driving away, one of the policewomen asked me if I was not saying hello to my friend. I told her I did not know anyone there and they started mocking me, saying I was lying. Then Carole said, 'Look, we don't know each other. This is the first time I have ever seen this woman.' I asked her who she was. She told me her name and that she had been charged with the same thing as me. I cried out and clearly remember saying, 'My God, but you're only a child!' She said she hadn't been at Guildford. I said I hadn't either, but that Paul Hill and Gerard Conlon had said things about me. At that, the police all started laughing.

When we got to Brixton, we had to go up a lot of steps to get to the wing which had already housed the Price sisters. In fact it had been opened specially for Marion and Dolours Price, who were tried and convicted of carrying out car bombings in London during 1972. They had only been moved out a few months previously. Although I was still dazed and shocked, I had been pulled out of myself a bit by the sight of this young girl who was on the same charge. She looked so young and helpless, and I think I unconsciously adopted her as my own daughter. As we went up the stairs with all these men in uniform standing around, it finally struck me—this was real, this was really happening to me. At the top there were another couple of wooden steps and then the door opened to reveal one self-contained wing with hardly a dozen cells in it. A couple of those were for the officers to sit in, a sort of staff room. As we moved along the row, Carole was in front of me. They put her in one cell and were taking me on to the next one when I saw some other officers coming towards me. I froze to the spot and begged them not to touch me, not to hit me any more. One of them said, 'We're not the police.' They assured me they were not going to beat me, that I was no longer in police custody, and put me into my cell.

I sat down and fought back a sense of claustrophobia that was to return every time I was locked into a cell during the whole of my time in prison. A few minutes later the cell door opened and I was asked if I would like a bath. I was still wary and didn't know what to say; I was wondering what they would do to me. When a young prison officer called Gloria spoke to me I just knew she was kind and gentle and genuine. She said she would run a nice hot bath for me. I felt all the better for it. Then I heard them taking Carole for her bath. At that stage, Carole was still a young girl and was not the easiest to handle. I think she was coming off drugs. She resented having done silly things in her past and not being caught—only to be punished for something she never did. But the officers were good with her and let her just sit alone in her cell when she was having a down day.

After we had bathed and were back in our cells, they brought a meal. I couldn't eat and asked to have a cup of tea. It was getting dark when the tea arrived, brought by male officers and in tin mugs. I always remember my mother keeping two or three of these tin mugs for when the tramps came around. I could never drink out of them or those plastic mugs in different colours they also have in prison. I told the officer I didn't want the tea, which was stewed thick in a bucket. 'I will do without, sir,' I said. I was still very polite and called them all 'sir' and 'miss.'

The next morning I still would not take any tea because of these mugs. I asked if I could have my own cup and plates. When one officer asked just who I thought I was, I told him I was Mrs Maguire and I could not drink out of those tin mugs. It went on for a couple of days and I think the doctor began to be concerned. You are supposed to be innocent until proven guilty, they say, and I think they were getting worried as we were on remand, not convicted prisoners. The doctor said I could buy my own teabags and that there was a kettle on the wing which we could use. My Aunt Teasy, who visited me every day while I was in Brixton, was told she could bring in a china cup and plate. We were still not allowed proper cutlery; we had to use the plastic prison knives and forks. I say 'we' because I always included Carole in my requests. One officer said I had fought hard enough for the privilege so should not throw it away then for Carole. But I said I would not take it if Carole could not have it too. How could I possibly sit down with my china cup and make my own tea and Carole not be allowed to? Our cupboard was soon well stocked up.

Before long the officers started to take their tea with us as well. I must say that in Brixton there were only one or two sarcastic officers and they didn't go out of their way to be particularly nasty to us. The majority were decent, and it was the little things they would do which touched you and made you feel you were a human being after all. When finishing their shift, some of them would get changed into their own clothes, come up to see me and say, 'How do I look, Anne? Does this suit me all right?' A small thing like that can mean a lot and keep you in touch with reality. And Gloria always did our hair. I looked like some frightful zombie until she cut my hair and got it back into good condition. She would also do our make-up for visits.

Christmas was approaching. I was thinking of how we had taken out our Christmas tree lights to test them, how I had been preparing. Now I was a mother separated from her children. What kind of Christmas would they have this year? I knew the youngest two, Patrick and Anne-Marie, were staying at my Aunt Teasy and Uncle Bill's, and Vincent and John were trying to keep the house at Third Avenue going as best they could.

And yet I still could not weep. I couldn't in the inter-rogation room, I could not cry—the tears just would not come. I didn't understand it. I was crying out inside, 'Someone help me, believe me,' but there were no tears. It was not until a priest came in that I found that release. The Catholic chaplain and I were seated at opposite sides of a table. He looked at me and I said, 'Father, I am not guilty. I haven't done anything and they've put me in prison. Father, what for? Why have they done this to me?' As soon as he put his two hands out and took my hands, the floodgates opened, the tears flowed out of my eyes and didn't stop for days and days.

The officers had told us that as we were on remand we didn't have to work, but Carole and I decided it would be better to occupy ourselves rather than just sitting in our cells. As we were now living there, it was our home and we would keep it as clean as we could. The Price sisters had been moved out a few months before, so the place was a bit dusty. They had also painted the cells we were in to pass their time. Carole was a good little cleaner and every day we washed down a different part of the wing. We scrubbed the place from top to bottom. The floor we polished over and over with 'Cardinal Red.' One day we were each handed a little piece of paper—our wage slip. When we read it, we both burst out laughing—it came to the grand total of fifty pence. I asked Carole where were we going to spend it—Selfridges (the upmarket department on London's Oxford Street)?

Since the priest's visit had unlocked my tear ducts I had become a real Magdalene, shedding rivers of tears. Every morning I would be scrubbing the floors with my tears pouring into the bucket. I think at times Carole must have got a bit fed up with my constant crying. When she had herself locked into her cell, supposedly because she was in one of her moods, it was probably actually to get a break from my constant weeping.

One morning the governor came onto the wing while I was scrubbing the floor with the tears flowing as usual. He said to me, 'Get up, Anne.' I stood up and wiped my hands. He said, 'Look, Anne, I know it's hard. You're a mother and it's almost Christmas. But you are not convicted yet; you have a trial and if you know you're innocent, it will be proved.' I looked at him through my tears and asked why they were keeping me in prison, why couldn't I go home to my children for Christmas? He replied that he didn't know, he could not give me that answer.

Christmas came and went. At least I knew the youngest two at Aunt Teasy's would have Christmas dinner, but it would still not be the same as being with their own mum and dad. But I thanked God they were with a relative. If it hadn't been for that, I don't think I would have come through. At that early stage, I probably would have starved to death. Not deliberately—I just couldn't have eaten. I would probably have died from a broken heart longing for my children.

A couple of weeks after arriving at Brixton, I was still in a lot of pain around my kidneys and tummy area. A woman doctor examined me. I told her about all the beatings and kicking I had received in police custody, and we agreed that they were experts and knew not to leave marks. As she examined me, I screamed with the pain. To cut a long story short, I ended up having to go out to a hospital for a gynaecological operation. At the hospital I remember being on a trolley being wheeled down to theatre. People were sitting around waiting to see doctors or visit people. I was surrounded by all these policemen, and those watching must have thought I was a VIP or Royalty. One old gentleman actually bowed as I was wheeled past! Ever after, during my time in Brixton, the officers joked about that—their 'royal' inmate.

After Christmas we went to court at Guildford for our weekly hearings, when we would be remanded in custody for another week. On the way there, we would see out of the van windows but people couldn't see in. It broke my heart to see women with their children going to school.

At the remand hearings, Paddy, my brother Sean, Pat O'Neil and Giuseppe Conlon, who were also being held in Brixton but in a different wing, would appear in court together. I had to go in with Gerard Conlon, Paul Hill, Paddy Armstrong and Carole Richardson, as I was on the same charge as they, that is, murder by having bombed two pubs at Guildford. I remember one day Gerard Conlon was joking around with a policeman, and the officer said to him that would be one more stripe on his wellington boot. He was making fun of Gerard—being Irish he must wear wellingtons and so on. I was angry that this young man, who had got us all into this situation, could sit in court laughing and joking. I turned to him and sharply rebuked him, asking him what was so funny about our sitting there, innocent victims of his stupidity, including his own father who was not a well man?

Paddy Armstrong looked over and asked me if I was all right. I had never met him until we all appeared in court together and Carole told me that he was her boyfriend. I never even looked at Paul Hill. I had no reason to look at him or speak to him. I had only seen him twice in my life: at the dance with his friend Gerard Conlon and then when he was shown to me in the police station.

At one of the weekly hearings, I think it was at the beginning of March, we arrived in the room we used to wait in before being called into court. The others had already been in. Paddy and Sean were shouting over to me that they had dropped the murder charge on me and that I would be going home. Carole and I, who were sitting next to one another on one side of the room, looked at each other. She asked, 'What about me? Will they let me out too?' A policeman told Carole to come with him. I prayed, 'Please God, let them take the charge off her as well.' They took her into a side room and, when she came out, she told me they had not only left the murder charge standing but had added a whole list of others. I had told the governor and officers at Brixton what Powell and Robinson had said to me—that if they didn't get me on a murder charge, they would 'get me on the gloves.' I also said this to the young woman prison officer who was sitting beside us. She said that if they had another charge against me, they would have put it on me by now along with the murder charge. As they hadn't done so, she said it looked like I would be going home. Another policeman came over to us. He was holding a book in his hand and started reading out that they had dropped the murder charge against me but were charging me with having had traces of explosives on my plastic gloves. The young prison officer just looked at him and shook her head. 'I can't believe this,' she said to me.

Paddy and the other men were sitting on the other side of the room and obviously didn't know what was being said; until they heard me scream, that is. For the next thing the policeman said was, 'We have your two sons down the road and are also charging them.' I didn't know which two sons, but I just screamed out, 'Please, sir, don't touch my children, don't touch my sons. They are English born and bred. Do what you want to me, charge me, but please don't touch my children.' Paddy and Sean jumped up to come over to me but they pulled them back. (I didn't learn until the next day, when Aunt Teasy visited me, which two boys had been arrested.) They had Vincent and Patrick down at Guildford's Guildhall and were charging them with having traces of explosives on their hands too. It took them three months to charge those boys. Why?

My three boys had all been arrested that same night in December. We had all been taken except Anne-Marie. They did their swab tests on John's hands as well as Patrick's and Vincent's. The conclusion I have come to is that they made a mistake between John and Patrick. John's name is 'John Patrick' and Patrick is 'Patrick Joseph.' It is my belief that they meant to take the two eldest boys, not the young boy, and made a mistake with the initials. But I believe if they had made such a blunder they could not go back on it. When they realized they had taken the young one, the thirteen-year-old, how could they admit a mistake? If they did, might people realize they had made one big mistake all the way along? To this day, my second son, John, says he wishes they had taken him instead of his younger brother. Even though John was not taken, he has lived in a prison without bars since the day we were arrested. We all suffered, but particularly John and Anne-Marie who were left on the outside.

That day they removed the charge they had laid on me, as they couldn't make it stick, but they added two other intolerable burdens. They charged two of my sons with something which, like all of us, they had not done.

EIGHT

I thought my sons must already be in prison too. I couldn't sleep that night back in Brixton. It was heartbreaking. I believed they were locked up with criminals. Was anyone harming them?

The next day, when my Aunt Teasy visited me, I learned that they had in fact been released on bail. They were going to try to get bail for me too. Vincent had just been going out to work when they arrived at our house on Third Avenue and told him he was being arrested and taken to Guildford.

Anne-Marie and Patrick were staying with my Aunt Teasy and Uncle Bill in Kennington. Patrick was still in bed when the knock came to Aunt Teasy's door. She opened it to find four armed policemen asking if Patrick Maguire was there. She said he was and that he was still sleeping. They wanted to know which room he was in and she said she would take them, but they insisted they would go alone to his room. Anne-Marie and Patrick were sleeping in the same room and both of them can still recount in exact detail how they were awoken that morning. Anne-Marie, not surprisingly, started screaming as four armed men told her brother to get dressed and took him away.

Aunt Teasy still says today that, judging by the expression on those men's faces, they had thought they were coming to take away a man named Patrick Maguire, not a thirteen-year-old boy. She asked if he could not at least have some breakfast before they took him away. They told her he would get breakfast later. That's another story. Whatever else they dished out to Patrick, it certainly was not breakfast.

Anne-Marie was due to receive her first Holy Communion in May, and I had often said to some of the officers in Brixton that I so much hoped I would be out by then. In our religion it is the most important day in a child's life and equally, of course, for the mother and father. I was sure I would be out for that occasion even though they told me not to build up my hopes. It was too important and God would not let me down.

A couple of weeks later at our usual remand hearing, the solicitor was going to present an application for bail. Paddy, Sean and Pat O'Neil were taken in for their hearing first. The court turned down their application. Then they took in Giuseppe, who was a sick man. They turned him down too. The prison officer accompanying me kept telling me not to build up my hopes as they had turned down all the men. I said no, I was going home for little Anne-Marie's first Holy Communion. By this stage, it was only about three weeks away.

Paddy's brother Hugh and his wife Kitty had moved into our house on Third Avenue, because John was rebelling at what had happened to us and was out of control. Vincent was older, and was always more sensible anyway. In court I saw that Hugh was there as well as my Uncle Bill. Hugh was called into the witness box and told the judge that he had no children of his own but was trying to look after John, and he didn't know what to do next, how to control him. What all the children needed, he said, was their own mother. After a pause, the judge said he could see no reason why Mrs Maguire should not be granted bail. The prison officer accompanying me grabbed my arm so tight; she could hardly believe it. I whispered to her, 'I told you God would not let me down,' but she shook her head in disbelief.

The judge said I would have to sign on at my local police station every day. I remember saying to him, 'Your Honour, I shall sign on as many times a day as you want me to. Just let me go home to my children.' He gave a little smile and said once a day would suffice. He asked me what timing would suit to sign on; what time did my daughter begin school? We agreed I would sign on at my local police station between ten and ten-thirty, seven mornings a week.

Now I had bail I could leave directly from the court. Each time you make a court appearance, they bring your belongings with you from prison. That morning as I was leaving Brixton, I spoke to Carole Richardson through her cell door. We had piles of stuff in our cupboards, between Carole's mother and my Aunt Teasy bringing things in to us, and we shared everything. I joked with Carole that she was not to touch my stuff until she knew I was away home. She said, 'Go on with you, you won't be back.'

My heart broke that day leaving her behind, just as it did again years later when I left Judy Ward behind at Durham. I remember how Carole and I looked at each other, our eyes filling up with tears. We had been there together, the only two prisoners on that wing, for four months.

As we left the court, Hugh Maguire, who had come in a friend's car, said we would go and get the boys from school. When we arrived Hugh told me to lie down across the back seat to hide, and he went away to explain and to ask the headmaster if he could take out Patrick and John. As they were crossing the playground I could see Hugh wagging his finger scolding them. They must have wondered what on earth was going on, what had they done now! Hugh opened the back door and said to them, 'Now, get in that car.' Patrick was first and of course he got the surprise of his life. He just threw himself on me. Then John pulled him away and they were vying with each other to give me the most hugs and kisses. We got back to Third Avenue and I made the boys' favourite shepherd's pie for dinner. When Vincent came in and saw me standing in the kitchen he had the same overjoyed reaction as his brothers. He just picked me up and swung me around the floor, 'Mum, Mum, you're home!'

Aunt Teasy had suggested I leave Anne-Marie with her for another day or two until I got myself settled down again, but by the next day I could wait no longer. I got a lift over to Teasy and Bill's. I will never forget that sight. There was my little daughter sitting on the outside steps playing with her doll. When she saw me getting out of the car, she nearly fell down the steps in her rush into my arms. With tears in her eyes and her little lips trembling, she asked if I was taking her home. I said of course I was. That night my children and I were all back together in our little house at Third Avenue.

I was home for Anne-Marie's big day. Trial date was finally set for 12 January 1976. Even then I was still not worried about the outcome. I believed justice would be done, the court would see there was no case to answer, and we would walk out of the court and begin to get on with our lives again. Every day I faithfully 'checked in' at the local police station. After I had left Anne-Marie at school, I would go to Holy Mass at the local church and beg God to help us, to give me the strength to get through this for the sake of the children. Only once or twice I was a couple of minutes late for 'signing on,' when the Mass went on a bit longer than usual. There was one officer at Harrow Road police station and if he hated anybody, he hated us. He was one of the few who wanted to see us locked away for ever. He threatened me that if I were late again he would have me back in Brixton in no time. Eventually I was to end up taking the police from that station to court over the violence meted out to John and Patrick, but that is another story.

At first, I would go over to Brixton to visit Paddy every day. During the week there was no queue, and you just had to knock on the door. The officers there were friendly and would shout, 'Hey, it's Annie back to see us again,' and would ask how we were doing, how the children were and so on. Because of the time it took and not least because of the cost, Paddy eventually persuaded me not to make the trek every single day. Later, people told me I could have had help with the expense of visiting my husband and relatives in prison. At the time I did not know that and we certainly had no help or visits from social workers.

My sister Mary arranged to come over from Belfast in the summer. I received permission from the police to go away for a week, so long as I continued to sign on every day wherever I went. I booked a caravan at Clacton for a week and we went there with our children. I went to the police station every day, and on my last visit the sergeant in charge shook my hand and said he hoped this whole business would soon be over for us.

The brief respite of a week on the coast over, it was back to daily life on bail. In many ways it was harder than being in prison. We had already been tried and found guilty by some sections of the media, and many people simply assumed we were guilty. What was most hurtful was being avoided in the street by people I had known previously and even people I had helped in the past. If someone did stop to speak, the moment they saw anyone else that they knew approaching they would start to edge away. People didn't want to be seen with me. After all, they had read in black and white that our home was a 'bomb factory' and that I was 'Evil Aunt Annie.' It must be true, mustn't it? I myself used to believe everything I read in the papers.

I was quite alone in all this. Most people preferred to look the other way, not to get involved. There were, however, few instances of outright nastiness. Once we did have a note pushed through our letter box—to the effect that we were nasty Irish terrorists who should hang. I had one or two unpleasant anonymous telephone calls and had to have my phone number changed.

Whereas there was no violence from the Harrow Road police when we were arrested—all that took place at Guildford—things changed when we were out on bail. Young Patrick had only to step outside our door and he was picked up by police in a van and beaten black and blue. For that year we were awaiting trial, not a day passed when they didn't abuse my child, on his way from school, on a message to the dairy or as he walked to or from his little part-time job in the shop across the road. They couldn't get Vincent so much as he was picked up every morning and dropped off every evening from his work. If he went out, it was just one night at the weekend with his uncle for a drink at the Conservative Club. But Patrick got it every day. Every week, sometimes twice a week, I had the man from the police complaints commission out. He was a gentleman but there didn't seem to be anything he could do. Once he asked Patrick if he had noticed the numbers of the policemen who had beaten him up and Patrick took him upstairs to his bedroom. There he had a wardrobe which he had painted white. All down one side he had written the numbers of the guilty policemen.

Often I would have to go to the police station to get him out when they had taken him there to do their beating. The last time I took two neighbours with me and they too saw the state he was in, with blood pouring out of his nose. We took him to hospital. The doctor said it was not the first time he had seen victims of that police station and asked why I didn't take them to court and put a stop to it. He said he would testify for us. I took his advice and we did take them to court. But they threw it out, said there was not enough evidence to prove anything. The doctor had somehow decided to go on holiday abroad that week and was not available to testify.

Another evening, John's girlfriend Maxine came rushing into our house screaming that they had Patrick outside. I ran out, and there outside our own house was the police van shaking from side to side as they kicked young Patrick around inside it. John arrived home from school. They threw Patrick out on the pavement, hauled John in and gave him similar treatment. I was practically demented. I banged on the van and screamed at them to stop. Maxine was still beside me. As they threw John out, they told me in foul language that if I didn't clear off double quick, they would have me in that wagon and back to Brixton. I was at the end of my tether. It was worse than any prison sentence I would later serve. Paddy even went on hunger strike and wrote to the Metropolitan Police Commissioner saying he would not eat until the beatings of his sons stopped. They stopped.

67

Nowadays I remember with shame how a neighbour, Iris, had told me once or twice how her husband, Peter, had been picked up by the police. She would maintain he had not done anything. I would argue that the police didn't just pick on someone for nothing. I know otherwise now and apologize to Iris and Peter.

Once again, Christmas was approaching. It was very difficult. Despite the police brutality I was trying to instil hope into my sons that British justice would prevail. Money was scarce. Aunt Teasy and Uncle Bill were very good to me but it wasn't easy. I began cleaning at a local shop. It only paid a few pounds but every little helped. My friend and neighbour Teresa Roache suggested I ask the social services for some help—perhaps they would give me some food vouchers for the Christmas period. She said she would come in with me. I found the idea difficult, never having asked for anything before, but Teresa persuaded me to phone. A young woman answered and I explained that my husband was in prison and I was finding things a bit difficult; could they help me to get over the Christmas period? She told me I should make a pot of Irish stew for my family's Christmas dinner. I was never rude to anyone, but that day I admit I lost my temper and told her if she were beside me I would let her know all about Irish stew!

When I came off the phone, I was shaking with a mixture of humiliation and anger. Teresa and I went over to the social services office. We met the young woman and I told her I didn't need her cocky advice. My husband had been wrongly imprisoned, we were victims of a miscarriage of justice, and this was the situation I had been reduced to. Besides, I had never made Irish stew in my life, because my mother had not liked mutton. The office manager appeared and asked what the problem was. I just burst into tears and told him my situation. He took me into another room and listened patiently. He told me he had read about our case in the newspapers, that there was no cash available but he could give me vouchers for the supermarket, which he did. It was he who told me that I should have had a social worker while my husband was in prison, that I could have had help with my fares all the time I had been travelling to Brixton. He also informed me that when our trial started I should go to a social service worker based in the Old Bailey (the Central Criminal Court in London) and ask for help with our fares to the trial.

As I have said, you never forget those people who showed kindness in those difficult times. Three such were different gentlemen I met on Christmas Eve on my way home from the supermarket. The first was Sean Tully who was with his son-in-law. They reminded me that a children's party had been arranged at the Conservative Club and told me not to forget to bring Anne-Marie along. Then each of them pressed a twenty pound note into my hand. Further along, I met a neighbour, Mr O'Brien. We passed the time of day and he told me he was going over to County Cork for Christmas that afternoon. I wished him a pleasant holiday and a happy Christmas. I was just taking my leave when he pushed two fifty pound notes into my hand. On my way home, tears ran down my cheeks—not because of the money but because of the thoughtfulness I had just experienced.

We were a full house again that Christmas as my sister Kathleen came over from Belfast with her two little girls. When she went home after the holiday, my sister Mary came with her baby Martin. She stayed with us the whole time of the trial. As she had the baby, she didn't come to court but stayed in the house. It was a great comfort having her there. During the trial she would take Anne-Marie to school and collect her. Her baby had his first birthday on 17 January 1976. Our trial started on the twelfth.

NINE

On the morning of 12 January 1976, the police came to my door again. They were offering to drive us to the Old Bailey, the Central Criminal Court in London, for the start of our trial. Despite their new-found eagerness to help us, I refused. It would only make things look worse than they were. I had been out on bail for so long, I was not going to turn up at court in a police car as if I were some dangerous criminal or as if I had tried to abscond. Patrick, Vincent and I took the underground to the Old Bailey, as we did every day for the next seven weeks.

We have to remember the climate in England at the time. I can't blame people for thinking the worst about us. The IRA had launched its vicious 'mainland bombing campaign' and there was an atmosphere of fear and revulsion, coupled with the desire that these people be caught and punished as soon as possible. Unfortunately that led to over-eagerness, perhaps, in some quarters, and they ended up rounding up and punishing the wrong people while the real culprits were never brought to justice. My name had been in the media during the trial of the Guildford Four, even though they retracted their so-called 'confessions' and claimed police brutality. There were headlines along the lines of 'My Aunt Annie taught me to make bombs,' and 'Evil Aunt Annie's bomb factory.'

The same judge who tried the Guildford Four would sit on our case and we would have the same prosecutor. Some people had suggested to me that we should try to have our case heard elsewhere than the Old Bailey, which I believe was impossible anyway, and that we should ask for a different judge and prosecutor. I did make the latter request and was refused. But that didn't worry me. I knew we had not done what they accused us of—I had never seen, let alone handled, explosives—and I believed British justice would prevail and the truth would out. In fact, I honestly thought that first day, that they would look at the evidence and say there was no case to answer and we could all go home free again and start to rebuild our lives. It was not to be.

We all had to sit in the dock of course. The seating order was the same every day after that. There was me first, then Paddy, Giuseppe and Sean. Pat O'Neil and my two boys were in the row behind. There seemed to be an awful lot of people in gowns and very official-looking. It is a bit awe-inspiring sitting in the dock of the highest criminal court in the land, but we were all determined to tell the truth and so felt we had nothing to worry about.

One of the first questions to arise was whether the boys and I would be allowed to stay out on bail. The judge granted that but said that, for the duration of the trial, we would have to eat downstairs in the cells at lunchtime. I had not even made up sandwiches because, as I said, I believed it would all be over quickly.

That first morning seemed to go quite quickly although, to be honest, I didn't understand, and often didn't hear, a lot of what was being said. Come the lunch recess, I was taken down to the women's cells. There were officers there who had brought prisoners in from

Holloway and other prisons. I actually knew some of them because they had been at Brixton. They said to me, 'Come on, Annie, get your sleeves rolled up and help us with these dinners.' So I helped them distribute the lunch trays to the other prisoners. Then they invited me to eat my lunch with them. I helped them again the second day, but there were some other officers there and after I had helped with the distribution they locked me in a cell. That was hard, that feeling of being locked in a cell again. But it was only for an hour or so, before I was taken back up to court.

The judge had decided there was a case to answer and the trial ended up going on for seven weeks, not helped by an outbreak of 'flu—me, Paddy and one or two of the jurors—causing a postponement for a couple of days. It became a routine for the boys and me, going in on the tube in the mornings and home in the afternoon. Proceedings would finish around four o'clock and I would often pop into a grocer's shop near the court to do some shopping. One time I met one of the court ushers, and the two of us walked around the store together with our baskets on our arms like any other two housewives. If only people knew the rather different situation we were in minutes before! She took a liking to my boys and actually bought them bars of chocolate before we left the shop.

In the first week of the trial, we were making our way home as usual on the underground when the boys told me that there were two members of the jury further down the carriage. I looked up to say 'hello' and saw a look of shock as they turned away. They got off the train before us. The next morning I stood up and said to the judge that I didn't know if it mattered but I had seen two members of the jury on the train the previous evening.

He smiled and said it was not serious but thanked me for telling him. From then on we were kept in half an hour after the jury to allow them to catch their trains in peace!

The trial continued day after day. In truth it was frustrating, and also very boring. We did not know what they were talking about half the time. The men tried to keep their spirits up for me and the boys. They were being transported to and from prison every day. Pat O'Neil was always a bit of a joker and he would say things to try to make us laugh. Young Patrick would bring his notepad and pass the time drawing. There was one Scottish officer there—he was the one who had taken me down to the cells that first lunchtime and said to the others I could help them with the lunches—and he took a liking to Patrick with him being so young. He would chat away and joke with him and was kind to both of the boys. When we were actually convicted, someone overheard him say he would never believe in British justice again. He had tears in his eyes and I think it broke his heart to see my two boys being put away. On the whole, we were lucky to have nice people like that dealing with us.

I had to go into the witness box. I think my evidence lasted two days. It was not a pleasant experience—especially when the prosecutor, Sir Michael Havers, was trying to tell me I was guilty because of the gloves. As he held them up, he asked, 'Are these your gloves, Mrs Maguire?'

I replied, 'If you say they are mine, if they are the gloves you took from my house, then they must be.'

'Answer "Yes" or "No',' he told me.

I asked him to let me see the packet of plastic gloves. He asked if I implied he was telling lies?

I told him I wasn't, it was just that I knew my gloves had the design of a hand on the packet.

When I was leaving the court that day, a professional person told me I should have replied that they were 'similar to my gloves,' that if I had said that I would have walked out of that court as they could not prove they were mine and I could not prove they were not. I do not know if that was the case and besides, I don't know how I would have coped with Paddy and the two boys locked up and me being on the outside.

The questioning went on and on, but I still wasn't worried. I wasn't afraid of contradicting myself or being tripped up because I was telling the truth and I thought that once the truth was out, they would see we were not guilty. I was still believing in British justice.

At one point there was a policeman in the witness box. The rubber bullet came up. He said that it had been sitting on my coffee table as an ornament. I couldn't hold back. I jumped up and said, 'Your Honour, he is telling lies.' I said it had been in a drawer in the back room and I had told the police about it that night they came to our house. He told me to sit down, as it was not my turn to speak. That really shocked me. Although I had had the bad experience of the police at Guildford during my 'interrogation,' I still could not believe that they could go into the witness box and take the same oath as me and then lie. My family and I were being branded as terrorists who killed innocent people and children, and the jury was believing it.

Of course, the weightiest 'evidence' against us was the now-discredited forensic test—TLC, or Thin Layer Chromatography—which purported to show that we had had minute traces of nitro-glycerine on our hands or, in my case, on my gloves. Years later, in a television documentary programme on our case, eminent professors of pathology at Glasgow and Dublin cast doubt on the validity or reliability of the swab tests done on our hands, on the strength of which we were convicted of having handled explosives. They demonstrated that other substances could give the same result. But in our case, they couldn't even do a later check as the original swabs had been either lost or destroyed at the government laboratory by the seventeen-year-old technician who had done the analysis. At the trial, the forensic expert who had invented the test even disowned it, saying that common household substances could have produced the same result.

I won't speak about the behaviour of the prosecutor or the impartiality of the judge. That has been done elsewhere, in other books. Anyway, the trial was reaching its end, and after the judge's summing up the jury would retire to consider their verdict. I had studied their faces over the twelve weeks and thought they were all reasonable people, who would not convict us. The judge said I would have to spend the night in Holloway, and the boys would be in custody too when the jury retired. That last morning as we were leaving Third Avenue I had a very heavy heart. I thought it was because I would not be home but in Holloway that night. As little Anne-Marie put her arms around my neck and kissed me, as she did every morning, I held her very tight and began to cry. She asked what was wrong and I said it was just that I missed taking her to school every morning as I usually did. I couldn't tell her I was going into prison that evening, even if it was only for one night. She would have panicked and become upset after the experience of separation we had already had when I was in Brixton. John was going out to work and, naturally, I had to tell him we wouldn't be home that evening. But we would be back the next day. That is what we all believed. My sister

Mary, bless her, who had stayed with me all during the trial, had planned a celebration dinner for our return.

After my night in Holloway prison, the jury reassembled on 3 March 1976. They returned 'guilty' verdicts. I was devastated. I spun round and grabbed hold of my boys and cried out, 'Oh no, not my sons, please.' Paddy took a hold of me and kissed me on each cheek. As soon as he released me, I turned to the jury and I admit I screamed at them, 'You're wrong, you're wrong. We are not guilty.' That is all I remember. At that point I passed out. The next thing I knew I was being carried downstairs. Then I remember I was lying in a cell. A male officer from Brixton prison whom I had known, and who knew Paddy and the men as well, was there. The tears were running down his face and he was patting my cheeks to bring me around. I heard him saying, 'Come on, Anne, you've got an appeal. You'll prove it at the appeal. Come on now, be brave for the boys' sake.' He was actually crying with me. There were two women officers there as well. They were all telling me I would prove it at the appeal. At that stage, I didn't even know what an appeal was.

I was the first to be sentenced: fourteen years in prison. And at that time, I thought fourteen years meant fourteen years, not knowing about remission. I didn't even hear sentence being pronounced on the others. I just passed out. To me fourteen years away from my children, fourteen minutes even, was a lifetime, an unbearable thought. Paddy received fourteen years as well, my brother Sean, Giuseppe Conlon and Pat O'Neil twelve years, Vincent who was sixteen got five years, and thirteen-year-old Patrick four years.

So I was going back to Holloway. Before they took me away, they let Paddy into my cell to see me for a moment but they did not let the boys in. Apparently Paddy and the others heard me still screaming as they were taking me out to the van. I was screaming for my children, they tell me.

Years later I was also told about the scene at our house when the verdicts were announced on television. John's girlfriend Maxine was the first to have heard it, and she ran into our house screaming that they had put me and the others away for fourteen years. My sister Mary collapsed. My good friend and neighbour Teresa Roache came over to help her, and eventually had to call out the doctor. Anne-Marie was hysterical. It must have been terrible.

I arrived back at Holloway. When they were admitting me, I had a cross and chain around my neck which the children had given me as a Mother's Day gift the year before when I was in Brixton on remand. The admitting officer told me to take it off. I just grabbed on to it, and holding it tightly said it was not coming off my neck, my children had given me that and I was not parting with it. She insisted all jewellery had to come off. Then, and I don't know to this day why I said it, I suppose my mind was not functioning properly, I said if they took that off me, I would die or kill myself.

That did it. They grabbed me and took me to be locked in a 'secure cell' for people who are deranged or mentally ill and might be a danger to others or to themselves. I begged them to leave me alone, but once in the cell they held me down on the floor and injected me with something. The next morning I was taken out into the van again to be transferred. They told me I was going to Durham. I didn't know where Durham was, I had never heard of it before. I couldn't remember whether I was in that van for twenty minutes or twenty hours, I was still doped with the injection from the day before.

I do remember that in the van a male officer had a newspaper and he was showing it to his female colleague. It was about me, their prisoner, and he was making sure I saw him pointing it out. On the journey at some point, we pulled into a service station, whether for petrol or a toilet stop I don't know. When I looked out of the window, the whole place was cordoned off, and there were police vans and cars and motorcycles everywhere. I was such a dangerous convicted criminal now, that I had a whole convoy of police vehicles and personnel accompanying me.

I was still a bit doped when we arrived at the prison. We stopped at some big gates and the driver spoke to someone through this contraption on the wall, the likes of which I had never seen. We drove in and the gates slammed shut behind us. This was Durham jail. This was my new home.

CHAPTER
TEN

Durham jail was an old Victorian prison with one wing
for women. The day I arrived, they had all been locked
in their cells and the wing was on top security alert. Not
only was Annie Maguire, a big bomber, arriving with all
her police escort, but they had also been informed by
Holloway that she was a potential suicide. Much later in
my sentence the wing chief and I laughed about that.
She thought there was some sort of lunatic arriving on
her wing.

I was brought into reception. Still doped up and weak-
ened, I couldn't walk but had to be carried in. A female
assistant governor said to me, 'Well, Annie, all your
friends are here and waiting for you.' 'What friends?' I
said, 'I don't have any friends here.' She was referring to
the other Irish prisoners—or 'Irish terrorists' as some
called us—Anne and Eileen Gillespie, Judith Ward and
Carole Richardson. They really believed we all knew
each other.

I was taken up to the sick bay, as they called it, and left
on a mattress on the floor. I am not sure how long I
stayed there, but am told it was over a week. I remember
going in and out of consciousness. I was screaming out,
not out aloud but inside, screaming and breaking my
heart. I cried non-stop that whole week and for many

weeks afterwards. I understood fourteen years to mean fourteen years; I didn't know about remission. What was going to happen to Anne-Marie and John? Where were Vincent and Patrick? Was anyone abusing them? How would they cope with prison?

After a couple of days, the authorities probably started to worry. I hadn't eaten or drunk and just could not stop crying. A Catholic priest came in to see me, Father McKenna. He tried to encourage me to get out of the sick bay, to be strong for the sake of my husband and children. He was also the first one to mention to me the names of Anne and Eileen. They were the Irish girls down on the wing and he said they would help me and look after me. The 'sick bay' was a row of tiny attic cells at the top of the wing. The chief officer on the wing, Chief Clough, would come to see me and try to speak to me as well, telling me I would feel better when I got out of the sick bay and down onto the wing. Much later, she said that when she went off duty that weekend she did not really expect to see me alive when she came back, such a condition was I in. In all her years in the prison service she had never seen anyone in such a state.

Another day I came to, to find a young girl trying to spoon-feed me. The first words I heard were, 'Come on now, Mother, get this soup down you.' Who was this calling me Mother? I wasn't sure if I was dreaming or hallucinating. There were two young women, and they laughed and introduced themselves as Anne and Eileen. They got me to take another few mouthfuls of soup and gave me a pep-talk. I was going to be strong for my family, they said, and we would have an appeal. Everyone kept telling me about this appeal, but it didn't mean anything to me. I just wanted out. Nearly every day in prison, I honestly kept expecting someone to come and say they had discovered it was all a big mistake, that I was free to go. Whenever the chief or an officer called me into the office for something, my heart would flutter.

Anne and Eileen's visit roused me a bit and I started eating again. What got me up above all was the news one day that my sister Mary was downstairs to see me. A nun from north London, Sister Sarah Clark, had called to our house after hearing the news of our conviction and sentences. A week later she drove Mary and Anne-Marie all the way to Durham to visit me. They had brought a big box full of fruit and sweets with them, and some tobacco, as Sister Sarah thought Paddy would be brought to visit me at some point and I could pass it on. The authorities told them, however, that I would not be allowed to receive their box of goodies. Sister Sarah and Mary asked them to pass it on in that case, as there was no point in taking it all the way back to London. The officer told me this later and I asked her if she could distribute it among the other inmates without telling them where it came from, which she did.

They didn't allow Sister Sarah in to see me as she was not a relative, but I could see Mary and my daughter Anne-Marie. Visits were in a room where the prisoner had to sit on the opposite side of a table from the visitors. There was to be no physical contact. When my little daughter walked in, of course I just swept her up in my arms. In fact, I was reminded of that moment when we saw those pictures of the Princess of Wales running open-armed to greet her sons after they had been separated for a week while she was on a foreign tour. We sat down with her on my knee, her arms tight around my neck. One of the officers guarding us during the visit rebuked me and reminded me of the rule. I looked at her and said, 'This is my daughter, she is only a child.' I didn't put Anne-Marie down.

Mary and I couldn't stop crying. She was almost passing out with the shock of seeing the state I was in, and my heart was breaking because I knew my daughter would soon have to leave me again. The whole visit was a terrible ordeal. The other young officer who was guarding us was fairly new to the service. She became so upset that she had to excuse herself and be replaced by another. She was to tell me later she had never seen a mother in prison in as much sorrow as me that day.

The visit came to an end. They had to tear my little daughter away from me. It would be months before I would see her again. I could still hear her screaming for her mummy as she was taken away across the courtyard and out of the prison. As I was taken back to my cell, I felt I just wanted to bang my head against the wall, I was so out of my mind with grief.

After another few days I was declared fit to go down onto the wing. Although I had been in prison at Brixton before, I was not then a convicted prisoner and only Carole and I were on that wing, there was no general prison population. I really didn't know what to expect now. When they took me to my cell, I couldn't believe my eyes. It had been decorated with flowers and fruit. I was standing looking around in amazement when some other prisoners came in. It was Anne and Eileen again, with Judy and Carole. A special bond was to develop among us five as we were 'Category A' prisoners—supposed high security risks—and so, of course, were treated differently from the others.

'Well, come on, Mother,' said the girls, 'are you not going to offer us a cup of tea?' I thought they were crazy. I told them I didn't have anything like that, and didn't think we were allowed to have such things in there. Anne said, 'Well now, let's look in this cupboard. I'm sure we'll find you can offer us a cup of something.' When she opened the cupboard there was tea, coffee, sugar, biscuits, and a flask of hot water which they had all donated. Their kindness was a good therapy as it got me playing the hostess. I had something else to think about for the first time since we had been sentenced. It also taught me that prisoners, whether innocent or guilty, are people too, as are the warders. Before my own experience, I had always imagined prison warders as big tough characters with lots of keys and big sticks. I found out that they weren't. The majority of them were just other women like me, going out to work to help support their families. And if you respected them, most of them respected and treated you properly. You quickly learn there are two ways of doing your time—the easy way and the hard way. If you respect the rules, do what you are told and treat the officers with respect, you'll get by. If you cause trouble, are uncooperative and cheeky you'll get the same back.

Once onto the wing, I had to adapt to normal prison routine. Mind you, we Irish prisoners were not treated as 'normal ones.' As 'Category A,' we had to be accompanied by two officers at all times. Our cells were apart from the others and could not be opened by any ordinary officer, only by special security officers. It would have been terrible if you were discovered sick in your cell, as Judith Ward once was, as it took them so long to get our cells opened.

We were moved twice within the space of my first month. That was very difficult for me because I would just have cleaned the cell from top to bottom, put my pictures up on the board and begun to feel it was my own space when, without warning, they would come along and move me. In later years I started writing down my experiences, until one day a spot search was conducted

Top right Me with my dashing boyfriend, Paddy Maguire

Top left Bathtime for our second (rather startled-looking) child, John

Bottom Mummy's parents Gran and Grandpa Clark

Top left I kept this photo o
my little girl Anne-Marie
pinned up on my cell
throughout my prison
sentence

Bottom Anne-Marie visits
Santa Claus with her cousin
in Belfast while her Mummy
is in jail in England

Top right She always put on
brave face while deprived of
her Mum and Dad. At nigh
she cried herself to sleep

Above Anne-Marie with her Grandad Smyth, my father. He died just after my release from prison

Left Now my daughter and I see each other every day. We cherish our time together

Patrick feels deeply for other victims of injustice. Here he supports a campaign for the wrongly-imprisoned Birmingham Six

Above Rather a faint picture of my visit, with Gerald Conlon's sister, to see Chris Mullen MP (second from right) at the Houses of Parliament

Below With my brother Sean, also arrested that fateful night at Third Avenue

Above As I was deprived of enjoying Anne-Marie's childhood, thank God I can now see her daughter, Lee-Anne, every day

Below My sister Mary, who stood by us through thick and thin, laughed when we came across this old tin bath of the style we were bathed in before a coal fire when we were kids

Above Mary and me on one of our pilgrimages

Below A relaxing moment during a pilgrimage to Lourdes. (Back, l to r) My sister Mary, His Eminence Cardinal Basil Hume, Me, Father Archie who had been chaplain at Durham, a family friend. (Front, l to r) Carole Richardson and Lisa Astin (*Sally McAllister*)

Above My younger two grandchildren, Lee-Anne and Patrick, are almost the same age now as Anne-Marie was when we were separated (*John Cole*)

Below I cherish the moments every day when the family all pop in. (Back, l to r) Patrick, John and Vincent. (Front, l to r) Lee-Anne, Anne-Marie and me with Patrick's son, Patric Maguire III (*John Cole*)

and my notebook was confiscated. Most of the officers didn't like this any more than we did. Not all of them, however. Some would have preferred that we be hanged rather than given a cell on their wing.

On the hour, every hour, the officers had to come round and check on us by lifting the little hatch on the outside of the cell door. I did find that annoying. If the officer on duty was one who did not like us, she would make sure you heard that hatch banging up and then banging down again. Thank God, there were only a few like that. They were the same when they were locking you into your cell at night. They wouldn't say 'Good night,' but would just bang the door as hard as they could. After a while, I started to tease them and would say, 'Make sure you close the door now!' Others, who were a bit more humane, would say 'Good night' and close the door easily without any need for useless banging. That was dealing woman to woman, one human being to another. What has happened to the rehabilitation aspect of imprisonment in England? If we just lock people up with other criminals and treat them poorly, can we really expect them to come out any better than they went in?

We were wakened at half past seven and our doors were opened at eight o'clock every morning. You had to be up and ready to come out immediately. If you weren't, they asked you if you were all right. If you were not, the door was locked again and it was reported to the chief, so no one wanted to miss that open-up unless they were really ill. It was bad enough being locked in the cell for twelve hours during the night, without having to spend any more time there than was absolutely necessary. Once the door was opened we had to 'slop out' and return to tidy the cell and make the bed. Chief Clough was very strict, and rightly so, about standards of cleanliness and tidiness. If any of the girls started to let herself go—her standards of personal hygiene, or the state of her cell—Chief would soon inform her, 'You are not in Holloway here.' Likewise, she wouldn't allow people to play radios in their cells loud enough to disturb others. It was her wing and she was determined that conditions would be the best they could be in an old and primitive prison. She did her best in the circumstances.

Breakfast, if you could call it that, consisted of tea with bread or toast and margarine. But, as with all our meals, it was prepared in the kitchen of the men's wing and left outside the door of our wing a quarter or half an hour before it was served to us, with the result that it was always stone cold. The breakfast toast was so hard as to be inedible without risk of breaking a tooth! We would normally just take tea and a slice of bread.

By half past eight we had to be lined up for our morning work shift. As was customary for new prisoners, I was put on cleaning duty for the first few months and the scenes from Brixton were repeated. I would be scrubbing the floors with my tears running into the bucket. We stopped at half past eleven for lunch—or dinner really, as it was the main meal of the day. That, too, was always cold by the time we got it. We had to queue up and pass down the line to be served. There were no condiments to make it any more palatable and the drink was always tea.

One day in that first week on the wing, as we were queueing, a young girl was standing behind me. She was a bit simple and leant forward and asked me, 'Will you be my butch?' I presumed 'butch' was prison slang for 'friend' and said of course I would be her friend, I wanted to be friends with everyone. She appeared delighted and off she went. For some reason, she took her meals in her

86

cell. As we sat down, the others asked me what she had been saying to me. They explained to me what kind of 'friend' I had agreed to be. They were all laughing, thinking it hilarious what 'Mother,' as they now called me, had assented to. I saw red. At that moment I think I snapped out of the daze I had been in and shot upstairs to the first floor where this girl's cell was. I stood at her open door and screamed at her never, ever, to say those things to me again. Of course, the staff heard me and ran to see what all the commotion was. They calmed me down, but the little girl, and the whole prison, had got the message. I would not be bothered that way again.

After lunch there was some free time when we could take a shower, write letters and so on. At half past one we lined up again for recreation. If it was not raining, we went out into the exercise yard, or 'the playground' as I called it. It was just a big concrete yard—no grass, no flowers, just concrete surrounded by barbed wire fencing and under the surveillance of cameras. Beyond the barbed wire, all we could see was the side wall of the men's wing. Sometimes they would be at their windows shouting over to the girls.

One day at recreation I saw what I thought was a workman climbing up a drainpipe on the side of the men's wing. Two officers always stood at each end of the 'playground' when we were outside and I pointed over, saying I hoped that the workman would be careful, as he was making a dangerous climb. The officers asked 'What workman?' and within seconds all the women were whisked inside. The 'workman' I had been so solicitous over was a prisoner going up to make a protest of some sort! I don't know how long he was on the roof but it caused quite a stir, with the local media all turning out. It also caused us to miss recreation.

The other Category As took great pleasure in winding me up. They had been there longer than I, and I believed everything they told me. Another day at recreation in the yard, I noticed a small 'plane flying around and around overhead. There had been a case of a prisoner escaping at some other prison in this way. I pointed out the encircling aeroplane to the prisoner who was walking beside me. I nearly died when she told me to be quiet, because it was coming for her. Any moment now, she said, it would lower down a rope and she would be off. I was terrified, envisaging the scene I was about to witness. I begged her not to do it. Then she added that I was going with her. My knees turned to jelly and my mouth went dry and I pleaded with her not to do it. I must have gone ghostly white because, when she saw the look on my face, she burst out laughing. I had been had again! However, the dutiful prison officers had also noticed the encircling plane, and we were once more whisked inside—another exercise period abruptly terminated!

I often laughed and shared a joke with the other prisoners and some of the officers, but the smile on my face was only skin deep. I made an effort to associate with the other prisoners and be sociable but I cried myself to sleep every night of my sentence.

On days when the officer in charge judged the weather to be 'inclement,' we were sent to the dreaded 'blue room' to do PE. The woodwork may have been painted blue, but our colour surely matched it by the time we came out. It was very cold and very, very damp. I still joke that my aches and pains date from the hours I passed in that blue room. It felt more like an underground bunker than a gym. As well as suffering the cold and damp, there was sometimes another problem. The windows of the punishment block looked into this room. If a prisoner, usually one of the younger ones doing their time the hard way, had got into trouble, she would be sent into isolation in a punishment cell. We could hear the screams and protests all during our recreation. Once, one young girl did a 'dirty protest.' She didn't use the toilet, but covered the walls of the cell with her own excrement. It was awful, but in that stench we were still made to do our 'recreation.' The smell was so bad that most of us were physically sick.

Thank God, I never landed up in the punishment block. Throughout my sentence, I was always correct, often having to bite my lip rather than react to comments that were made to me about terrorists who should hang or suchlike. I was determined they were not going to add another day, not even another minute, on to my sentence. No one would provoke me into saying or doing anything which would keep me away from my children any longer than was necessary.

Sometimes there were PE competitions to keep the girls motivated. One day Eileen Gillespie won the prize. She was really fit, full of energy and good at the tasks set. As she was receiving her prize, her sister said, 'If only Mum and Dad could see her now.' My eyes filled with tears as I told her that perhaps they couldn't see her, but at that moment I was as proud of her as any mother could be. They were so young that I really did consider them and treat them as I would my own children. I even became quite good at the PE myself and once won a badge—until I had my operation, when I had to stop doing it.

After recreation, it was back to work. After about six months, I was assigned to the workshop where we made sheets, soft toys, whatever contracts we could get. We were even asked to make uniform trousers for the male officers. Of course, interest in the workroom went up and it seemed all the women were volunteering for duty there so they could measure the young officers! Once more in my life I was back on a sewing machine, but not in circumstances I could ever have imagined when I was a young girl in the factory in Belfast. Eventually I graduated to being the 'checker'—or what on the outside would be called the 'quality control officer'!

When the afternoon work session was over there was the evening meal. A lot of people on the outside find it difficult to believe the 'feeding times' on the inside. Your main meal is at half past eleven in the morning, and your evening meal at half past four in the afternoon! If there were chips or anything barely edible, we would eat it. Often the meal consisted of a cheese and potato pie and other pie-style dishes. The baking trays must never have been very well washed over in the men's kitchens, because the bottom of the pie would be absolutely filthy. We would remove the pastry and put the remainder between two slices of bread to make a sandwich. At Durham, I suffered terribly from mouth ulcers, sometimes having two massive ones in my mouth at the same time, making it impossible to eat. At times the pain was so bad I wept. The doctor said it was due to lack of vitamins. Aunt Teasy offered to pay for me to have vitamin tablets but they refused. She even offered to pay for another doctor to give a second opinion, but that too was refused.

After the evening meal there was 'association,' when you could mix with the other prisoners or take part in any classes that were organized. At half past seven we had what they called our 'bedtime tea'—a cup of prison tea and a bun. Then we were locked in our cells. The cell contained my bed and a half-wardrobe with a little writing table attached, under which was a cupboard. As we were Category A high-risk prisoners, there were three sets of bars on the window. Each night I fought an engulfing sense of claustrophobia as that cell door was banged shut.

Sister Sarah, who was tirelessly determined, along with my family, to remind the outside world that we were still alive, once printed a postcard, headed '14 years 1976 INNOCENT DURHAM 290718,' with some of my lines on it.

As I lie upon my bed my window opened wide
I hear the winds roar aloud
I see the rain bursting through the cloud
A light shines through onto the wall
That faces my bed
The reflection of the bars I dread
Now I know what it is like to be alone
In a prison cell on a cold, cold winter's night alone.

CHAPTER
ELEVEN

I didn't see my husband and two imprisoned sons again until seven months after our conviction. Other prisoners and some of the staff had told me I could apply to have a 'family visit,' which I did. The prison governor, the chief officer and most of the staff were, on the whole, decent and fair. The delay appeared to be caused somewhere in the Home Office, which was awkward and unhelpful through our imprisonment. I even suggested it would be easier and cheaper to the prison service to take me to see Paddy and the boys—I was just one person—rather than transport the three of them from their respective prisons in the south of England up to Durham. But apparently I was too much of a security risk, being a wicked convicted bombmaker. What they conveniently forgot was that if I had wanted to abscond, flee the country or evade trial, I could easily have attempted to do so while on bail awaiting trial. However, now I was behind bars I was a 'security risk.' It should have taken a couple of weeks or months at the most to grant permission and arrange a family visit.

I had made the application through the prison governor. When he was doing his rounds and I was on my knees with my scrubbing brush and bucket, I would look expectantly at him. He would shake his head sadly and say, 'No news yet I'm afraid, Anne.' Then one day he approached me with a big smile and said he did have some news for me—permission had been granted for a visit from my husband and sons.

They were temporarily transferred to Durham men's wing. In fact, once they were all there, the boys did not know their father was also there, and vice versa, until one morning when they were slopping out and Vincent happened to look over the railing. There on the landing below was his dad performing the same task. Word spread around the other women and they started collecting sweets, biscuits, tobacco to send over to the boys. Once a week there was a 'canteen day' when you could buy these luxuries from the money you had 'earned' in prison. The women made up a big bag of goodies for the boys, and I asked the governor if he might take them over to the other wing for them. He saw that there were cigarettes for Patrick and said to me, 'He's a bit young to smoke, isn't he?' I looked at him and said, 'If he is old enough to be in prison, he's old enough to smoke, sir.' I would never have allowed him to smoke on the outside but, after all he had been through, I was not going to make a fuss about some cigarettes, especially if it helped calm his nerves.

Because we were all classed as such high security risks, everything was kept quiet. How I came to know they were there and that we were about to have our visit was that one day the wing chief said to me, 'I suppose you'll be washing your hair tonight, Anne.' That was her way of letting me know something was happening, and she knew I would want to look my best to see my husband again. I did wash my hair and the next day other inmates gave me some make-up and helped me look my best.

Visits in prison are always difficult. Normally, of course, the visitors are coming from 'outside.' The visitor tries to tell the prisoner only good things so as not to worry them, and the prisoner does likewise, trying to show that she is all right, her spirits fine and so on. As a result, there can often be little true communication and certainly the prisoner will go away and cry her eyes out afterwards. I experienced it and saw it happen time and again in my years in prison.

The time arrived to meet my husband again after seven months' separation. I was so nervous. What would it be like? Would we be able to speak freely? Some of the officers were as excited as I was. I was taken to the visit room and they brought Paddy in. Of course, we ran into each other's arms. When the duty officer told us to separate we sat demurely at opposite sides of the table. There were four officers, two male and two female, standing over us. So much to say, so many experiences to relate, so many thoughts and worries to share about our family, those outside and those locked up like us. How was it possible to tell it all? We could hardly speak, choked with emotion. I shed rivers of tears. At one point, Paddy unthinkingly took my hands in his. We were immediately rebuked and reminded that there was to be no physical contact. Instinctively, I withdrew my hands from his. Paddy got angry and told them this was his wife he was visiting, an innocent woman who shouldn't be in prison. I told him to calm down and not to take it out on the officers, as they were only doing their job.

After another few minutes they brought in my boys, Vincent and Patrick. Patrick, a boy in a man's prison, was wearing prison clothes which were way too big for him. He had to hold up his trousers with one hand the whole time to prevent them falling down. He looked a pathetic little waif and was embarrassed having to see his mum like this, holding up his trousers. They said they didn't have any clothes in his size. That night, when he did his rounds, I asked the governor if he could not find better-fitting clothes for my son. He did. The next day I saw them, Patrick had different trousers on. They were still far too big, but nothing like as bad as the other ones.

After that, we were supposed to see each other at three-monthly intervals, but I only saw the boys once again with their father while they were in prison. The hassle of being transferred from their own prison at Wormwood Scrubs and having to stop overnight at a different prison en route, in both directions, was too unsettling for them. Of course they visited me when they were free again. I say Paddy and I were 'supposed to' have three-monthly visits because it seemed to me there was someone, or some persons, in the Home Office who revelled in making as many difficulties as possible for us, and we never knew when a visit would actually take place. For example, I still have a copy of a letter from the Home Office to my then MP, Arthur Latham, explaining why we had not had our visit in April of 1978.

It is not always possible to arrange their visits at exactly three-monthly intervals because of the heavy demands on the limited amount of secure transport available to the prison authorities... The next visit after January fell due in April but (...) it was not possible to transfer Mr Maguire to Durham then because of the industrial action the Prison Officer's (sic) Association was engaged in.

The visit did not happen until 7 June that year, that is five months after our previous visit.

The whole procedure of trying to arrange visits was a frustrating one. Because we were Category A high-risk prisoners, we could not receive visits at the same time as the other prisoners or as each other. As a consequence, my visits had to be planned well in advance, and often I had to wait a long time to get a date for them. This also put a strain on my family who were, of course, having to travel fair distances to come to see me. Once my Aunt Teasy phoned from London to arrange a visit and was told it would be six or eight weeks before she could have a date as the visits were all booked up.

There was one small visiting room. In it was a desk as you came in and behind that a little table on each side of the room with two chairs on either side. When 'ordinary' inmates were having visits, they would put in other tables so that four prisoners could receive visits at the same time. We Category A high-risk prisoners could only have visits one at a time. Anne and Eileen were sisters so they had their visits together, fortnightly. It was not their fault, but the week they were having their visit, no other prisoner could have one. If Judy, Carole, Anne, Eileen and me could have had visits in the same week, the other week would have been left free for the ordinary prisoners. But someone in the Home Office did not see it that way. The tension on the wing over this issue was so great at one time that I feared there would be a riot.

This sort of thing didn't help the atmosphere in the prison. I don't think that the other prisoners actively disliked us Category As, but because of the sort of restrictions our presence imposed, it did sometimes make things more difficult for everybody. Another possibility would have been to use another larger space, perhaps the workshop, at least for the ordinary prisoners' visits—but that was not allowed either. Our impression was that the

Home Office really wanted to punish us. Some prisoners blamed the governor or the officers, but it was not their fault. Some officers even admitted to me that it was a sick situation and did not make their job any easier. If Chief Clough could have run that wing the way she wanted, it would have been a lot more humane. She cared for her inmates and took her responsibility for their wellbeing very seriously.

My sister Mary, who was such a brick right from the beginning of our troubles, made the journey over from Belfast at least twice a year. She had three young children of her own plus Anne-Marie to look after, and would bring some or all of them with her. On each occasion, Mary would make an exhausting 'pilgrimage' around the four or five different prisons we were held in. While it was great to see one of my own and to see Mary's selfless dedication, those visits were also painful. It was clear how much my sister was hurt by what had happened and was still happening to us. Despite my best attempts to put on a sunny front, she could see clearly the pain of her younger sister wrongly imprisoned and separated from her children. We shed many a tear during and after those visits. One time Mary broke down and asked the prison staff if she could not serve part of my sentence for me! That's sisterly devotion for you.

Mary and her husband and family made tremendous sacrifices in order that she could make these gruelling journeys on her 'prison trail' to visit us all. Once she arrived at Durham only to be told at the prison gates that she couldn't see me—the prison officers were having industrial action, work to rule or something like that.

I remember one visit when Mary brought Anne-Marie to see me. It hurt very much. At the time my daughter was living with Mary and her husband and family in

Belfast. An organization which worked for reconciliation by bringing the children of both communities together on holidays invited Anne-Marie to go with them on a trip to Canada. When she came back she brought a pair of earrings for me as a gift. The duty officer wouldn't let her give them to me. Another officer was upset by that and pointed out that she could at least have accepted them and put them in my property to avoid hurting the child.

Another time they came to Durham after there had been another terrorist outrage. Mary, coming from Belfast, had the accent. She had to walk around the town's bed and breakfast establishments seeking someone who would accept her. When she and Anne-Marie were about to take a taxi to the prison, the driver asked if they would mind sharing with a couple who had been waiting at the same time. She said she wouldn't mind at all. Once they heard her accent, the couple announced they were not prepared to sit in the same car as Irish scum like her. If anyone has merited their reward in Heaven, I think it is my sister and her husband Hugh. They stood by us through thick and thin. Surely their Lord will say, 'When I was sick or in prison, you came to visit me.'

One time, I think it was about 1979, Mary and Hugh came over to England for their regular 'prison pilgrimage' and went to see Paddy who was at that time being held in Hull prison in the north-east of England. They had Anne-Marie and John with them, and as they presented themselves at the door for their visit they were told that they could all go in—except Hugh. The reason given was that he 'had not been cleared for visits.' Hugh pointed out that he had indeed been 'cleared' and if they cared to check they would see that he had visited Paddy in Bristol prison before he was transferred from there to

Hull. The officers told Hugh that Bristol prison must have forgotten to forward the appropriate papers and Hugh was not admitted to visit. As Mary took Anne-Marie and John in to see their dad, Hugh had to sit outside the prison.

It was a bad time for us 'Irish prisoners' when there had been another terrorist outrage on the outside. It was as if we were on the outside and personally responsible for the attack in the eyes of some officers and fellow inmates. We dreaded the reaction whenever we heard news of another bomb going off somewhere. Anne and Eileen and the others can still tell the story of how one prisoner barricaded herself in her cell when Lord Mountbatten (a cousin of the Queen's husband Prince Philip and last Viceroy of India), was murdered sailing his yacht off the coast of Ireland, as she didn't want to mix with 'those IRA women.' If people really believed we were convicted terrorists, it is not difficult to understand. I can't blame them.

I remember very well my first Christmas, of 1976, in Durham jail. A carol service was arranged and there were to be visitors from outside attending. I think each officer could invite one or two family members to come along.

As a mother, I was used to being fully caught up in all the preparation for the Christmas feast, to make it as special a time as possible for the children. Although every Christmas in prison was hard for me, that first one will always stand out in my mind. At home, I often used to sit with my children in the run-up to Christmas, teaching them different Christmas carols. Like so many people, the song 'Silent Night' was our favourite, our special Christmas hymn. Well, at our carol service that night in Durham, with all the staff and visitors assembled along with the women prisoners, they opened with that carol, 'Silent Night.' It was too much for me. I broke down and could not stop crying. In my heart of hearts I knew that if I, Anne Maguire, was in a prison that night it should have been as one of those visitors, going back home afterwards to my husband and family. They stopped the singing and Chief Clough led me out and into the bathroom which was situated on the ground floor. I think I even cried out as I was being led away, 'But I am an innocent woman. I shouldn't be here.' Anne and Eileen said that even as they took up the singing again, as loud as everyone tried to sing, they could still hear my sobs. Some of the officers said that many of the visitors were in tears too that night, never having seen a prisoner in the state I was in.

Like other mothers, the officers were doing their best to prepare for their family Christmases too, often popping out to do a bit of shopping in their lunch break. I would overhear their chatter as they discussed how their preparations were going, and what they were planning to give their children as gifts. One day just as I was coming out of my cell, I glanced over the railing down to the ground floor. An officer was coming in from her lunchtime shopping carrying a great big teddy bear. I did an immediate about-turn back into my cell. The pain in my heart was so intense, the longing to be with my children so overwhelming that no tears, no words could give vent to it. Yet again, I wanted to bang my head on the wall and knock myself out, anything to blot out this engulfing grief. I had had a glimpse of myself in years gone past. It would have been me, struggling along carrying parcels and presents, hiding them before the children came in from school. The officer in question must have seen me dashing back into my cell and later came to see me and apologized. I told her it was not her fault; she was just doing her Christmas shopping like any other wife and mother. It was just that I found it all so difficult to bear. I knew the truth. Why wouldn't the police and the courts believe me?

On Christmas Eve, just before lock-up, we were all out on the landing wishing each other 'Goodnight' and 'Merry Christmas.' Once we were in our cells the assistant governor came round to give her seasonal wishes to everyone as she would be off duty the next day, Christmas Day. I actually had my head under my pillow in an effort to stifle my uncontrollable sobbing. I knew Anne-Marie and John were all right because they were with my sister Mary. I say 'all right' but of course any child would prefer to spend Christmas with her own mum and dad. It was Vincent and Patrick I couldn't get out of my mind. They, too, would be lying in a prison cell somewhere alone this Christmas Eve. The assistant governor must have come to my door but I did not hear her. After she had finished her rounds she came back to my cell and had the door opened which, as I said before, was quite a procedure. Along with the night officer, she came into my cell, sat on my bed and tried to console me. I don't think she was a mother or married herself, but she did try her best. She spoke about the appeal which we would have to prove our innocence. But it was impossible. No matter what words anyone spoke, or what they might have offered to give me, all I wanted was my family. When I repeated my usual refrain—that I hadn't done anything, that I should be at home with my family—I don't know if she believed me or not, but she sort of nodded her head sympathetically.

She asked if I would like something to help me sleep. I just did not trust anybody after all that had happened to me. I had never been a person for taking pills or medicine if I could help it, and after my experience at Holloway, I didn't fancy taking any chances. I was afraid they might dope me up and put me in isolation again. During my first year in prison I was still 'finding my feet' as they say. I was learning the routines and conventions and who was who. As new prisoners were 'sussing out the officers,' so they too were 'sussing out' their new charges.

On Christmas morning we were woken up by the bangs on our doors at the usual time. As I came out of my cell I was not quite with it, I had cried so much during the night. The other girls told me, 'Look on your door, Mother.' There was a knob handle on the outside of our doors—nothing of course on the inside, just flat iron from top to bottom. On the knob was a paper bag. Judith Ward and some of the other young girls had prepared little 'Christmas stockings' for us all, with some sweets and an apple and an orange inside. They had also made little Christmas cards; mine had big lettering on it saying 'Anne' and 'Mum.'

Beforehand, the other girls had told me that they had been allowed parcels in from their families the previous Christmas, so I asked my family to send me in cigarettes to give to the other women. We all gave our parcels in to the office and all the contents were pooled. The sweets were all put into one big box and all the cigarettes and tobacco into another. During the day they would be distributed to the inmates. Another inmate was there at the time who is dead now. I don't know if she was innocent or guilty, but her case involving murder had made headlines. She was very good to me when I was first in prison, and said that if I was given those long thin cigarettes, then I could give them to her as she liked them.

She also had prepared a little gift for me; talcum powder. I was not in any state to think about it that first year, but I later learned that in the run-up to Christmas, officers would buy little things like perfumed soap and talcum powder outside on behalf of the prisoners, things which were not available in the prison 'canteen.'

Another prisoner, who had herself once been a prison officer and had got involved in an escape attempt with a prisoner, also went out of her way to be nice to me that first Christmas. She had bought and wrapped a little gift and she said to me, 'I truly believe you are an innocent person, Anne, and if you know yourself that you've done no wrong, then you keep strong for the sake of your family. One day you will prove your innocence.' This was more of the kind of warmth and thoughtfulness which I had not expected in prison and which did help me.

At breakfast we had been treated to a piece of bacon. At half past eleven we had our Christmas Dinner. They even had menus printed out; if the public had seen them they would have thought we were being spoiled. But they needn't have worried. It was so bad, I wouldn't have given it to a dog. We tried to eat some of the roast potatoes and vegetables but the 'meat' was not fit for human consumption. I don't know what it was, but it certainly was not turkey. Afterwards we were allowed to put on the record player, and the young girls let themselves go, dancing like crazy to use up their energy. Those who wanted to were allowed to watch television.

Anything which helped relieve the boredom of the monotonous prison routine was welcome. There were only a few evening classes at the beginning—English, Spanish and a make-up class. We prisoners knew each other for the people we were. But the poor teachers who came in from the outside only knew that some of us were

'Category A' convicted terrorists. They were petrified, the officers told us later. Some teachers even refused to come in when they heard that 'IRA terrorists' were there. They didn't seem to bother, though, that such and such a prisoner, an infamous mass-murderer, was there. An officer once told me that she got so fed up with a teacher asking her what we were like, that she said, 'Oh, Anne Maguire has two big horns coming out of her head, actually!'

One week it was announced that there might be a sewing class and all those interested were invited to come along the first evening the little sewing teacher came in. It was clear the poor woman was nervous. Some of the girls sensed this immediately and decided to play up. As we had to introduce ourselves, they would say, 'I am So-and-so and I am here for murder' or, 'My name is Such-and-such and I'm a convicted terrorist.' The poor little teacher turned whiter and whiter. Her hands started to shake more and more, so much that she could hardly write down our names. The mischievous girls thought it was hilarious, but the poor little teacher never came back!

The others persuaded me to go along to the make-up class one evening. 'Come on, Mother, it will do you good,' they said. In truth, they were probably trying everything to prevent me sitting in my cell weeping of an evening. A mischievous fellow inmate introduced me as 'Anne Maguire, the convicted IRA terrorist.' Once more the poor teacher went ghostly white and began to shake. In the end, however, we became good friends and I thoroughly enjoyed her classes. When she was leaving, she actually said to me she looked forward to the day when she would hear my innocence proved.

One evening a group of us were sitting in my cell chatting over a cuppa, and everyone was talking about what they were learning in their classes. One prisoner suddenly said that since there were now classes in English, French and Spanish, why didn't we ask for a class in Irish? I thought that was a bit much and didn't think they would allow us to do it, but the others, including a Libyan girl and other English and Scottish prisoners, said they would be interested. Anne and Eileen Gillespie were bilingual and normally spoke to each other in Irish. The authorities had tried to stop them communicating in Irish but eventually gave up. I agreed to be the spokeswoman and put in the request. The duty officer was a bit bemused but, once he learned how many were interested, said he would see what he could do. After consultation, and probably checking it with the Home Office, he told me some days later that they couldn't get a teacher in but could provide us with language-learning cassettes.

The others used to laugh at me. It didn't seem to stay in my head at all, however hard I tried. The officers would chuckle as well. As they did their rounds to check on us in our cells, they would ask me if I was listening to my cassettes. I did find it difficult to concentrate as my mind was constantly on my family and wondering how they were all coping. I was practically ready to give it up as a bad job. One day I was on the ground floor with Anne queuing for dinner when Eileen leaned over the upstairs railing and, in Irish, asked what was for dinner. I replied in Irish that it was roast potatoes. Eileen said something else in Irish and I, stumped for an answer and rather than let the side down recited the 'Our Father' in Irish—which sent Anne and Eileen into hoots of laughter. At this a prison officer ran out and told me to come into the office immediately. She told me I was never to speak Irish on that wing; it was not my language and I was not to use it. I remonstrated that we were learning it and surely the point was to practise. She was adamant—I was never to speak Irish on the wing again. That was the end of my linguistic adventures!

We were allowed to continue using it in one particular circumstance, though. We had set up one room as a little chapel which the Catholics used for Mass and the Anglicans also used for their service. The prison chaplains were a great support to me. First there was Father McKenna, then Father James. Another was Father Archie, whom I met again when I went on pilgrimage with Carole Richardson to Lourdes after our release. But we had the impression that the chaplains were moved on or changed whenever they showed signs of becoming too involved with the 'Irish terrorists.' What the authorities didn't seem to understand was that there were certain things I could only speak to a priest about, just as there were matters I would only speak to an officer about, woman to woman. Anyway, in the chapel, some of us would say our evening prayers, the rosary. As Anne and Eileen had grown up saying their prayers in Irish, the officers allowed us to continue doing that.

After a couple of years I learned that our appeal had been turned down. I heard it from another prisoner who had seen it in an evening newspaper. It was rejected at the Old Bailey on 29 July 1977, even though members of the infamous IRA unit, 'The Balcombe Street Gang,' confessed at their trial to having committed the Guildford bombings. One of them said, 'I refuse to plead because the indictment does not include two charges concerning the Guildford and Woolwich pub bombings. I took part in both, for which innocent people have been convicted.'

It later came out in a book by Grant McKee and Ros Franey (*Time Bomb*, published by Bloomsbury, 1988) that the original list of indictments against the Balcombe Street 'Active Service Unit' of the IRA had included charges dating back to August 1974. When they came to trial in 1977 (that is, after we had already been imprisoned) a refined charge list 'referred to no offence before December 1974.' The authors of that book stated, 'For some reason the Crown had no desire to link the men in the dock with bombings in Autumn 1974. Certainly the explosions at Guildford and Woolwich were conspicuously absent from both sets of charges.' These men had confessed to committing the crimes of which we had been wrongly convicted. The same book quotes Sir Peter Imbert (who was connected with our interrogations at Guildford and later became Metropolitan Police Commissioner), from *The Times* of 12 July 1988, as saying, 'Oh, I believed the Balcombe Street Gang all the way through...'

Understandably, the loss of the appeal set me back quite a bit, affecting my morale badly. Another particularly difficult time was Giuseppe Conlon's death on 23 January 1980. When I heard that he was very ill and had been hospitalized, I asked permission to visit him but was turned down. Giuseppe died still a prisoner and protesting his innocence with his dying breath. I did not sleep that night when I heard the news on my little radio alone in my cell. I thought to myself, 'Giuseppe, you were a gentle, peace-loving man. You didn't deserve to die in these circumstances.' And I vowed that night that I would be strong, that I would do all in my power to clear all our names—for the sake of the Conlon family, for Pat O'Neil, my brother Sean as well as my own husband and children. Also for my children's children. I didn't want them having to live with the name Maguire as a stigma. The cycle of suffering caused by our being wrongly accused and convicted would have to stop some day. The truth would come out, if I never stopped campaigning until the day I died. And even though it might prove uncomfortable to a lot of people, and make us question our whole British system of justice, I would not remain silent for the sake of all those others who may have been wrongly indicted and are languishing in prisons for crimes they never committed.

I suffered another setback in the summer of 1981. In March of that year my brother Sean's son, Sean Smyth Jnr, married his sweetheart Christine in Belfast. Six weeks later it was discovered he had cancer and he died on 11 June. Understandably, his young widow was heartbroken and young Sean never lived to see the beautiful daughter he and Christine had conceived in their short married life. My brother Sean was refused permission to go to his dying son's bedside and, like myself, was refused permission to attend the funeral. He was allowed one telephone call to his family on the day of his son's funeral.

The fact that I would not express remorse for my 'crime' meant that I would not be eligible for parole, that is, early release from prison. Various people had recommended I apply for parole. When I asked what I should do they informed me I had to write a letter expressing remorse for my crimes and promise not to do it again if I were released early. Of course I couldn't do that as I had committed no crime. Some officers continued to encourage me, and I began myself to think that I must try. I figured if I did not try every channel open to me, I would never be able to face my daughter again. So I wrote to the Parole Board, telling them honestly that I had not done what I had been accused of, but was asking their good offices to be released from prison as soon as possible for the sake of the children who needed me. Parole was not granted. The situation was the same for all my family and all the Maguire Seven; not one of us expressed remorse for something we knew we had never done. And none of us was granted parole.

The only time I was outside the prison gates during the eight years I served in Durham was in 1979, when I had to go to hospital for an operation. I was still having 'women's troubles' and the prison doctor called in a gynaecologist who recommended I have a partial hysterectomy. He asked how many children I had. When I told him, he said I could at least be happy to have four fine children. By the time I was free again, he said, I would be too old to have any more children. Therefore I had nothing to lose by having this operation. Why go through any more suffering, he said, when I already had enough on my plate? I found it very difficult to accept. I loved children and when we were arrested Paddy and I had been hoping to have another baby the following year, 1975.

It was arranged for me to be taken out to hospital in Newcastle. Again, people must have thought Royalty was on the move with all the police cars and cycle outriders that accompanied me. I couldn't believe it when I saw a helicopter continually coming in low in front of our car. I even asked the officers with me what this idiot thought he was doing? They told me the helicopter was there because of me. I thought it a complete waste of public money.

Again when we reached the hospital, there were so many police around it was more like a police station. I was put into a side room off the main ward and told to undress. 'No way,' I said, 'as long as there are policemen parading up and down past my window.' The sister didn't believe me at first but I assured her that, though I had been locked up for a while, I wasn't at the stage of seeing things! The police worked three shifts—a male and a female officer were constantly with me. In fact, I spent most of the night chatting to them. The next morning I had to go to theatre. A security officer from Durham and a policewoman came in with me, at least until I had the anaesthetic.

When I was given the pre-operative injection which makes you drowsy, I thought, 'This is it. No more little Anne-Maries, no more little Patricks, Johns, or Vincents.' I thought I was saying this to myself but apparently after I had the injection, I started crying and repeating aloud the names of my children. The young security officer who was accompanying me later told the chief it was a sight he would never forget. We had hardly spoken before, but he became very friendly towards me after that. When I was moved back to prison, he was one of the first to come and see me. He tried to comfort me. I remember he told me I had three strapping sons and a beautiful daughter while some people had no children.

Back at Durham I was placed in the 'sick bay,' the row of attic-like cells on the top floor. Later they had to take over these cells just to accommodate the growing number of prisoners. The gynaecologist actually accompanied me back to prison in the ambulance and saw me settled into my 'sick cell.' He called in again later the same evening. He said I was to have lots of drink and plenty of fruit and nourishing food. It was like the first day I went onto the wing again—the girls had had flowers sent in and bought fruit and orange juice. There was a sister and a nurse who were OK, but another nurse who obviously did not like us. Once I asked her for a drink of juice as I needed some more liquid. She replied sarcastically, 'Well, your friends are keeping you, aren't they?' I had seen other 'ordinary' prisoners being given that sort of thing automatically while on the sick bay, and here I was being told to buy my own or have 'my friends keep me.' But we could not speak out. I could have been put on report and, as I've said, that was one thing I was not going to allow to happen. We suffered any injustices or indignities in silence. You just had to bite your lip.

CHAPTER
TWELVE

One of my favourite programmes on television now is an Australian-made soap called 'Prisoner Cell Block H,' all about life in the fictional women's prison of Wentworth. I feel I can identify all the characters in that series. One of them is an old dear called Lizzie.

We had our own 'Lizzie,' an old lady who was constantly in and out of prison—'an old lag' in prison parlance. She was not too steady on her feet and you would hear her shuffling along even if you didn't see her. She was in and out a couple of times while I was at Durham. One day I heard the shuffle and turned around to see 'Lizzie,' looking a bit older and frailer. When I asked her what she was in for this time, the officer who was accompanying me turned away and I was sure I could see her shoulders shaking. 'Lizzie' told me she had 'been done' for trying to hold up a jewellery shop, not for the first time. Like me, you may think such a crime is no laughing matter but I, too, had to laugh when she told me what she had been 'armed' with—a water pistol!

The scenes in my favourite soap where all the prisoners are bored and thinking of things to do, remind me of one Easter weekend in Durham. I should say that if I prefer to remember funny things we did, it's because in fact the conditions there were so dreadful, especially during the first years. We did daft things to give ourselves a laugh and guard our sanity. But prison life was no bed of roses.

Easter weekend was approaching—I think it was in 1978—and the workshop was due to be closed on Good Friday and Easter Monday. We were asked to propose ideas for different activities over the holiday weekend. Because our wing was such a closed environment with little activity and so few classes, we made the most of any occasion that was given to us to do something different and have some fun. People came up with different ideas and one prisoner, a 'lifer' who had newly arrived on our wing, suggested an Easter bonnet parade. Everyone thought it a great idea. Even the officers joined in the spirit and brought in crepe paper, bits of cardboard and the like, to allow us to make up our 'designer creations' with paper flowers and various decorations.

The evening after the decision had been made to hold the bonnet competition, this 'lifer' and I were sitting in my cell knitting and chatting about the upcoming parade and how we were going to design and produce our hats. The Gillespie sisters came in and we all continued discussing different ideas. Then Judith Ward came in. When Judy was in good form, she would laugh so much. I was thinking that someone should go as a film character, for example Audrey Hepburn playing Eliza out of *My Fair Lady*—one of the younger ones—and I wondered out loud if they would let us wear a wig. Well, Judy went into kinks of laughter and was practically rolling around the floor. Of course, part of the reason I was in prison was because of those two wigs, 'incriminating evidence,' found in my house. I had to see the funny side of it!

Anne and Eileen finally decided they were going to use one of those big plastic dustbin lids, covering it with silver foil and decorating it with paper flowers and ribbons. I was impressed by their idea but still had not come up with my own design. Once the young ones left to begin executing their designs, my fellow knitter said that I was going to go in the parade and she had an idea for me. I asked her what it was and she just kept looking over at my net curtain.

The previous Christmas my Aunt Teasy had given me a net curtain with a rose pattern on it. At home it was the sort of thing you would put on your bathroom window, but on my cell window it became a little rose garden. As the view out of my window was a concrete wall, through three sets of bars and an iron mesh, it meant a lot to me. I told my fellow inmate there was no way anyone was going to cut it. She assured me we would just fold and tack it. I was to enter the Easter bonnet parade as Mrs Shilling of Ascot hat fame! Gertrude Shilling is famed throughout Britain for her appearances at Ascot races ladies day each year wearing the most outrageous hats designed by her son David.

We got a piece of card from the officers. Chief had said we could use old torn sheets which were no longer of use, so we covered the cardboard with pleated sheet material, then with my pleated rosey curtain. Chief lent me two silk roses, little rosebuds and two satin streamers. She even lent me one of her own evening dresses and two strings of pearls. Another officer brought me an umbrella to use as my parasol, a young Libyan prisoner did my make-up, and Anne and Eileen put my hair up. I must say, it took years off me and I felt as if I were in my twenties again. We had such a laugh and it gave us a real lift. The judges were to be completely neutral, not officers or anyone who knew us, so a panel of three people from 'the outside,' probably friends of the staff, was to be invited in to judge our Easter parade.

We had a buffet lunch that Easter Sunday. I was full of the joy of the Easter feast. The priest came to celebrate Mass in our makeshift chapel and we determined to spread the joy of the occasion. To me, the Lord had risen and it was a time of great joy. We did our best to give all the prisoners a lift from the normal prison routine. The great moment came for our Easter parade. I thought to myself, 'What on earth am I doing? What if my children could see me now? Here's me, Anne Maguire, a mother of four children, used to going out to all my cleaning jobs, parading around like some fashion model—in a prison!'

But parade around we did, to great applause and hilarity. The judges awarded me first prize. I would have given Anne and Eileen first place for their marvellous dustbin-lid creation, but they got the second prize.

Later we held a dance. The priest and even the governor came to it. We had great fun watching the young ones doing all their jiving. They had such energy! Chief had brought in lemonade—a great treat as we were not normally allowed even to buy that. We were also given an extra half-hour before being locked in our cells: half past eight instead of the usual eight o'clock. I think after all our games and activities, everyone went to bed exhausted that night. But wake-up was still at the same time next morning. We were all joking about the morning after the night before and our hangovers—we weren't accustomed to drinking lemonade! That Easter with all its fun and activities helped me get through that year in Durham.

Another occasion which could have come out of 'Prisoner Cell Block H' was when we painted the entire wing. Work in the workroom was in short supply. We had finished most of the contracts and were waiting for some more to come in. So to prevent the girls getting bored, some of us had the idea of re-decorating the wing. It was Victorian-style, with a central hall going right up the four floors, and rows of cells down the two long sides of each floor. We asked Chief, who put it to the governor. He was apparently quite surprised, as this had never been done by women before. We assured him that we were capable of doing it and would make a good job. Everyone mucked in and was assigned specific duties. The high parts of the great gable walls were done by men from outside, but the rest we did ourselves. We suggested that different cells might be painted different colours apart from the usual ubiquitous, bland prison grey. I said that if the girls had input about the colour of their cell walls it would encourage them to take even more pride in their cells and keep them spotless. My argument was accepted and we were allowed to use various pastel colours.

Later on, when I was briefly transferred to Risley prison in Cheshire so that Anne-Marie could visit me when she was staying with her auntie in Manchester, I took up my paintbrush again. (I had so few visits at Durham that I 'accumulated' the right to many. I was able to go to Risley and let Anne-Marie visit me, and have many more visits in my last year in prison at Cookham Wood.) Not being content just to sit in my cell and read books during my fortnight at Risley, I noticed again the cell was a bit dingy. The staff were amazed at my repainting suggestion, but I assured them that we at Durham had done our whole wing and made a good job of it. They found this to be true and I duly 're-decorated' my cell again.

Another occasion when we had a special buffet lunch at Durham was for a joint celebration. First, Myra Hindley—a long-term prisoner infamous for her part in the 'Moors murders' with Ian Bradey, when they had lured and killed innocent youngsters in the sixties—had succeeded in passing exams and gaining some degree or other. Some of the prisoners were not happy we should mark that event but, as I said to them, they still ate the food, didn't they? Second, it was in celebration of a young prisoner's twenty-first birthday. Another lunch marked some anniversary of the Queen, perhaps the thirtieth anniversary of her accession. We were all given a little picture of her as a souvenir of the event. To the chagrin of some of the other prisoners, both English and Scottish, that photo went on my pinboard. We were not allowed to put posters or pictures on the walls of our cells but we each had a pinboard. In the centre of mine I had put a picture of the Sacred Heart of Jesus. It's a devotion which is often not understood but which represents the merciful love and tender care of our Divine Saviour. I've always liked that verse from Luke's gospel where Zachariah speaks of 'the loving-kindness of the heart of our God.' So the Sacred Heart was in the centre, and around him I put photos of my family as if to entrust them to his loving care. The photo of the Queen went there too. I sympathize with her as she has seen the marriages of her children break up, and she clearly loves her grandchildren, as I love mine.

As I've already said, I'm anxious that people don't get the idea that life in prison was all laughs and fun. It wasn't. Especially at the beginning, conditions were atrocious. Things only began to improve slightly and gradually after the arrival of Myra Hindley on the wing. She seemed to know prisoners' rights and get things moving. So whatever other prisoners said about her, we should at least have been grateful for the little benefits her presence brought for all of us.

In 1982 when I was still in Durham, Pope John Paul II made his still-remembered pilgrimage to Britain. In England he came north to Manchester and York. Anne-Marie was living in Manchester at the time and she and her cousins had camped out all night in order to see him. On her next visit she told me, 'Mummy, he looked straight at me and blessed me.' Whether he just looked in the general direction of where she was, I don't know. If nothing else, I thought it was quite significant—because of what had happened to us and everything she had been through in her young life—and it brought her great comfort and hope.

When His Holiness visited Ireland in 1979, shortly after his election as Pope, I remember Anne and Eileen were upset because they would certainly have been there along with their parents to see him. I know that a lot of people in Northern Ireland were hurt that he was not allowed to visit the North of Ireland, but who could ever forget his heartfelt plea when he spoke near the border, begging the men of violence to put down their guns and turn to Christ?

My sister Mary told me all about it when she next came to see me. I said I didn't suppose he would come back again when I would be on the outside but that, please God, when I was free I would one day make a pilgrimage to Rome and would see him there. That is a dream which I hope will be fulfilled one day. If I met the Pope I don't know exactly what I would say, but I think I would just take his hand and say, 'You believed. Thank you for remembering us.'

Just before the Pope's visit, I had a letter from Sister Sarah Clark, who had always stood by us since we were wrongly convicted. She had written to His Holiness telling him about us being in prison and the miscarriage of justice. She had obviously had some sort of response. She wrote and told me that when he came north to Manchester he would give a message—he was going to mention the prisoners nearby and he would specify the innocent and the guilty. I told this to some of the other prisoners and to some of the officers. On the actual day, 31 May 1982, we were all watching the visit on television. I admit most of us were in tears. For those of us who were wrongly convicted, we felt we were sitting in a prison watching our chief pastor on TV when we should have been out there celebrating with him. When he spoke, he said just what Sister Sarah said he would. His actual words were, 'In the Gospel Christ identifies Himself with prisoners when He says "I was in prison and you visited me." And remember that He did not specify whether they were innocent or guilty.' The other girls were overcome as well and I showed them the letter Sister Sarah had sent me.

One day the officers came in and told me they had passed some sort of vigil being held at the prison gates on their way in to work. It was a whole group of people, men, women and children, holding banners reading, 'Anne Maguire is innocent' and 'Release the Maguire Seven,' as well as banners drawing attention to the other wrongly convicted prisoners. Those officers told me it was so peaceful and beautiful that they wished I could see it. Now I did not, and do not, know who those people were. They held their vigil more than once during my imprisonment. It gave me hope and encouragement that at least we had not been completely forgotten, that some people believed we were telling the truth when we consistently maintained our innocence.

I never bore hatred to those responsible for our situation. That would be pointless. From day one I forgave.

I believe unforgiveness is like a sickness, a cancer that eats away inside you. If I had not forgiven, I would be a sick woman today. People continually ask me how I could remain without bitterness after all we have been through. I have to say it's because of my faith. Faith doesn't mean that everything becomes easy, but it does mean that you have hope.

So, prison life, like ordinary life, had its highs and its lows. I never ceased praying, nor believing that one day our innocence would be proved. I thank God for all those—family, friends, and people I have never met—who stood by us and believed in us. A Mr and Mrs Devlin and others in the northern English town of Bolton started a campaign for the Maguire Seven and the Guildford Four. One year, they produced an Easter card with a little poem I had written on it. It shows my anguish better than I can now:

> *As I sit here alone*
> *In a prison cell that's now my home*
> *My thoughts turn to years past*
> *And I ask myself*
> *How long will this torment last?*
> *I am innocent—*
> *Wife and mother—cry out*
>   *Oh Lord why me, why me?*
>
> *Husband, sons and my brother are alone*
> *For a prison cell is also their home.*
> *Five innocent people we be*
>   *Oh Lord why me, why me?*
>
> *If only you could take my hand and say*
> *Sit down Anne, and I will make you understand.*

When you see the tears I shed
Do you, Lord, remember the tears your Mother shed
When they put the thorns around your head?
  Oh Lord why me, why me?

Like the cross, my heart is heavy
And the load is hard to bear.
I say all the prayers that I was taught
And my love for you is always there.
  So Lord why me, why me?

THIRTEEN

Over the years of my sentence, I had to watch my children grow up without their parents. Like any other young people, they would have their problems to face but, unlike others, they had to do so with no mum and dad around. They had the added problem of constantly having to face people on the outside as 'convicted terrorists,' or the relatives of such.

Suffering, of course, is difficult to quantify, but we all share the belief that the two members of the family left on the outside suffered most, and probably John more than anyone. To this day he wishes that he had been taken. Like anyone, he finds it difficult to understand why they took his little thirteen-year-old brother and not him.

John went over to Belfast with Anne-Marie to his Auntie Mary after we were imprisoned, but when he couldn't find work, came back to London. He was left alone in the family home which he bravely tried to maintain for as long as he could. Aunt Teasy and Uncle Bill, along with Mary and Hugh, paid the rent. Uncle Bill kept popping over to check on the house. Once, when he was away the house flooded. Our carpets and furniture were ruined. Another time the house was broken into and the gas meter raided.

Uncle Hugh helped John get a job in the auction house where he worked himself, so he earned a wage and at the same time educated himself a bit in the antiques market. It also meant he was not hanging around the area we lived in all the time. He was constantly being confronted with his family's 'crime.' People could say some nasty things but he always told them we were not guilty and tried to walk away.

A year after we had been imprisoned, on 20 August 1977, he and his girlfriend Maxine married. I thought they were a bit young at eighteen, but nevertheless was not too worried as they had known each other for a long time. I thought that at least John would not be alone and would have someone to look after him. Eventually the local council moved them from our house and into a smaller flat. The local authority wrote to Paddy and me several times in prison, and persuaded us to give up our tenancy on our house on Third Avenue with the assurance that they would rehouse the boys and us on our release.

John and his wife invited Anne-Marie to come over from Belfast to live with them. Although she was very well cared for by her Aunt Mary, of course she was happy to go and live with her own brother back in London. John and Maxine had a baby boy, Jonathan, a year and a day after their wedding, and I will never forget the visit of my first grandchild in prison. Unfortunately the marriage didn't last and John was left a single parent, though greatly helped by his mother-in-law.

Struggling on a single wage to pay his rent, meet his bills and bring up his son, John still looked after his little sister as best he could, as did the other boys when they were released. Each of them had to save up to pay the fares to visit their dad and me in our respective prisons at different ends of the country.

As Anne-Marie grew up, I could sometimes see on her visits that all was not well with my little girl. But I didn't want to waste our precious visiting time by appearing to lecture her. Visits were so scarce that we both wanted to savour every moment of being together. Only now, as we sit and talk some days, is the extent of her hardship and suffering becoming apparent to me. I still find it hard to bear and weep whenever I realize all that she went through. Although John was good to her and got her up for school and so on, she still had to come in to an empty house after school every day. She was tormented constantly by other children about her mum being a 'bomber.' That little schoolgirl had to wash out her one set of school clothes each night for the morrow. If she'd had her mum and dad, that would never have happened. I know she has not told me half of it as she does not want to cause me any more pain. John and Anne-Marie were not taken that dreadful night of 3 December 1974, but nevertheless were orphaned and lived as in a prison without the bars. I suppose that's why I tried to advise the young prisoners who came into Durham.

Eventually I persuaded Anne-Marie to go and live in Manchester with her Auntie Anne, Paddy's sister. Although Anne and her husband treated her as one of their own, Anne-Marie still wanted to be with her own brothers and ended up going back to London. I couldn't condemn her for that. In the face of adversity, I suppose it is natural to want to be with your own nearest and dearest. Yet I worried constantly about all of them. I knew they were good and sensible kids, but it couldn't have been easy being forced to be adults and householders before their time.

I still have a few of the regular letters Anne-Marie wrote to me while I was in prison. Often she would draw little pictures on them, taking great care with the colouring-in. One of those was a drawing of herself showing me her new hair style. But what still strikes me about that particular drawing is that in it she is holding a big bunch of keys, as if unconsciously she is saying that if she had it in her power, she would open up those big prison gates and take me out. Or it may be that whenever she thought of her mummy, she thought of locks and keys, as she certainly saw plenty of those on her visits.

Her letters were always heartwarming and I would read them over and over again. They revealed not only her child-like innocence but also her ever-present desire to be with her own mum and dad again, and her attempts to be positive, to present a bright picture and encourage us in our ordeal.

Dear Mum,

I was really pleased to get your letter and I am very happy to hear that you are happy with the letters that I sent you.

December 1978

...I am doing well in school and my Christmas tests are coming up so I'll need to keep studying hard. I want to do well and every time I say a prayer I find the tests easier. I am still praying hard for you all that you will soon be out of there. I think God will listen to me even more if I really concentrate on my prayers, so I'll keep hoping and praying.

October 1979

...Never mind, Mum, I'll always have somewhere nice to live when you and Dad come home. But for now I've got to learn to settle down. Without you beside me, I know it is going to be hard but if that is the cross I've got to carry for God, then I will.

November 1980

From a letter headed in capitals,

I LOVE YOU MUM ALWAYS!...I love and miss all of you. Maybe one day these people will use their common sense and free you as they have no right to keep you there and they must know this deep down inside. Give my kind regards to all the girls and to the nice prison officer who is on duty at our visits.

June 1981

Dear Mum,
I hope you are well and not working too hard. I am still fine but every day I miss you more and more, knowing that when I get up in the mornings you are not there, and again at night. I suppose if you had done something I would understand. But it's so hard knowing that you have done nothing but been a good mum and wife. I can't understand why you are being treated as you are. I don't mean that the people inside are mistreating you, I mean by putting you behind bars for being innocent. But one day you'll be free and we can be together.

June 1981

And from a letter to Paddy which he has kept,

...I hope you are well, Dad, and saying your prayers because I'd like to be with you all again, even though Auntie Mary and Uncle Hugh are like a mother and father to me, I'd like to be with you again. But it won't be long and when you do come home there will be a nice big, big party waiting for you, so keep praying to God, and we will be together again.

When we were first imprisoned, Vincent was in Wormwood Scrubs as a Category A prisoner while Patrick was in Ashford, also Category A. I petitioned for the boys to be placed together and eventually they were.

126

I learned only recently that they were held in different wings, but at least they could see each other from time to time. Patrick was released from prison in March 1979. He actually asked if he could remain in prison the extra few months until his elder brother would be released as well. The Home Office wrote him a dry note informing him his request could not be granted.

When people think of all the publicity that surrounded the release of the Guildford Four, the Birmingham Six, Judy Ward—which was deserved and justified—they don't realize that my sons were turfed out of the prison gates having served their sentences, to no social workers, no press or TV cameras. They were still classed as convicted terrorists and had to try to get on with their lives as best they could, without the comfort of even having their parents or a family home.

Patrick stayed with his Uncle Hugh and Aunt Kitty when he was released as did Vincent, until our local housing authority gave them a flat together in a high-rise block. The social services were not very helpful. I had seen other prisoners going out to fully furnished accommodation, but Vincent and Patrick had nothing at first; no furniture, no carpets, nothing. With the help of their Uncle Hugh and brother John they began to get little bits and pieces and started making a home for themselves.

When Vincent was released he managed to get a job as a cook, having obtained his City and Guilds certificate while in prison. Anne-Marie used to love going down to Vincent's kitchen to meet him when she came out of school. He did that for almost a year before he left to take up a job as a labourer with the Electricity Board, where he stayed for ten years.

Once all the children were visiting me at Durham in early 1980. Patrick was keeping very quiet and seemed to be a bit fidgety. I asked him if there was anything wrong, but he assured me everything was all right. One of the officers on duty was Mrs Barr. Joanie had joined the prison service just at about the same time as I was sent to Durham. She was a lovely person and one of those who treated you as a human being. I used to tell her never to leave there until I was out of prison, as she was such a kind person—one of those who made the ordeal more bearable. In fact she did leave the prison just after I was transferred. The boys had brought photos to show me and, as was normal, had to pass them to the officer first. Joanie looked at them and cooed, 'Oh what a lovely baby, and just born too!'

I looked at John. 'No, not me, Mum.'

I looked to Vincent. He had a big grin on his face, 'Not me, Mum.'

I looked at Patrick. Surely not my youngest son? He was just a child when we were separated. He nodded his head sheepishly, saying, 'Yes, a little girl.' My little boy was a father! They knew both Paddy and I were always strict with them in their upbringing, and he must have been terribly nervous about my reaction. But how could I be angry with him, or any of them, after all they had been through? Once he got over that initial hurdle and saw that I didn't explode, he soon became his usual animated self and showed me all the photos as he told me about his little baby, how he had been present at the birth, how he loved to bathe and feed her. I had four children when we were arrested. Now here they were growing up—and I was a grandmother for a second time. Once he had broken the news, Patrick and his girlfriend would bring the baby to see me in jail and they would send me photographs every week, as I avidly followed the progress of my first little granddaughter.

My free time was once again used for knitting baby clothes.

In 1982 Vincent got married. I asked if I might be allowed at least to go to the church, but was turned down. All the family from England and Belfast was there. That day was one of the hardest of my sentence. I'd had two sets of rosary beads sent in and had them blessed by the priest. I said fifteen decades of the rosary on each one and sent them to Vincent and Kathy with a letter regretting that neither Paddy nor I could be with them on their big day. Although their mum and dad were in prison, I asked them never to be afraid to share any problems with us, that if there were something practical then, if we couldn't help them in our present situation, we could ask one of their aunts or uncles to act in our stead. As the day of their wedding approached, I was terribly upset. They were being deprived of their parents yet again, punished for something none of us did. Chief Clough and the staff must have realized the effect it was having on me, and the prison nursing sister asked if I would like to have something to calm me. I was never one for taking pills or medicines if I could help it, but that day I did. She gave me a tablet and I said another fifteen decades of the rosary for my son and his new wife before falling asleep until the next morning.

Paddy and I were decategorized just before Christmas of 1983. One day at recreation in the 'blue room' I was called to go to the governor's office. Category A prisoners were accompanied everywhere by two officers and a black book which held our details. As I entered the governor's office, the first person I saw was Mrs Barr. I instinctively greeted her with 'Hi Joanie!' but then noticed that the deputy governor was also in the office. I had to cover my tracks quickly if I wasn't to be put on report for familiarity with an officer or insubordination. I hastily corrected myself. 'I mean good afternoon, Mrs Barr. Good afternoon, sir.'

He asked if I would like to sit down. At that I went weak at the knees. In such a situation, my thoughts went straight to my family. I immediately asked him to tell me what was wrong and he assured me it wasn't about my family. He started telling me he was, 'very pleased to be able to inform me that...' I looked at Joanie who just bowed her head. She probably knew what my reaction was going to be. The deputy governor continued to tell me this wonderful news—that I was no longer to be classed as a Category A prisoner. Perhaps the poor man expected whoops of joy but I just looked at him and said, 'Oh really?' There was I, an innocent woman who had spent eight years in prison for nothing, and he was 'announcing a great joy'; that I was no longer 'Category A, top security.' I confess it left me unmoved.

He said I didn't seem especially pleased and then told me that Paddy had also been decategorized. I said only, 'Thank you very much, sir,' and walked out. I had walked into that office accompanied by two officers and the omnipresent black book. I walked back to the 'blue room' accompanied by only one officer. The other prisoners observed immediately that I no longer had my usual two-man escort and started cheering and clapping and hugging me. I felt nothing. To my mind they could have decategorized me years before, as they had Carole and Anne and Eileen. Of course I was delighted for them at the time, but it also showed the persistent attitude on the part of the Home Office towards me and my husband. If I were such a high security risk, why had I not done anything all that time when I was out on bail awaiting trial? If I were really in the IRA, why had I turned up of my own free will with two of my children for trial at the Old Bailey? I prefer just to put it down to stupidity rather than malice or ill-will on the part of the Home Office. Anne and Eileen and Judy had been relieved from 'categorized' visits in 1982. At the time I had been surprised that I hadn't been as well, since we 'Irish terrorists' were normally all classed together. It meant, of course, that they could have visiting under normal prison conditions. Why did the Home Office not do the same for me? They knew I was the only one among us who was a mother and thus had more need of visits. Even the officers could not understand the treatment I was receiving from the Home Office. Perhaps it was because of my attitude to the Parole Board. I knew I had to apply for parole for the sake of my family, but could not in conscience tell a lie by expressing remorse for something I knew I never did. Perhaps that is what hardened their attitude towards me; I don't know.

Paddy was due for release in 1984. I had to serve a year longer than he because I had been out on bail for a year before the trial while he had been detained in custody. He asked the Home Office if I could be released at the same time as him. When they refused, he asked if he could stay in prison the extra year until I would have served my time and be released. He couldn't bear the thought of his coming out of jail and his wife, an innocent woman, still being behind bars. His application was turned down and he was released in February 1984, one year before me.

Having been decategorized, in February 1984 I was transferred from Durham jail to Cookham Wood in Kent. It was still a prison but wasn't as bad as Durham—particularly the food! Recently I saw Durham prison on a television programme presented by Anne Diamond. I would hardly have known the old place. The cells are now what they call 'self-contained.' That is, each cell has a toilet. The women's wing, it seems, has been fitted with bright new kitchens. These are all things we never had and, inasmuch as we could, fought for. I am pleased that conditions may be a bit better now, but to be honest, I still think that the whole wing should be pulled down. It's old and there are always going to be problems maintaining it, as we sometimes had the sewers overflowing and gurgling around our feet on the ground floor. More than that, it is, in my opinion, outdated. It was designed and built at a time when the prison population was much smaller, and when people held a very different idea of what prison should be about from what most people would think today.

The most striking aspect of Cookham Wood was that there was grass and greenery and vegetation everywhere. For eight years at Durham the only piece of nature I had seen was when I was being whizzed to hospital in Newcastle with all my police escort. There at Cookham Wood you could see and touch leaves and plants at recreation. After Durham, it was almost heaven!

As I was being led to my cell, carrying my bedding and belongings, other inmates were doing their usual cat-calls, wolf-whistles and crude remarks, generally trying to be intimidating to this new arrival. Hands were coming out and trying to grab bits of my belongings as I struggled along behind the officer. It was intimidating and I was quite frightened. It was a very different atmosphere from the one I had known at Durham.

One of the first people I met was our dear 'Lizzie,' the old recidivist I had known in Durham. She put the word round that I had come from Durham, a 'hard' prison with its lifers, other long-termers and poor conditions.

The attitude of the other inmates changed immediately. I went up even further in their estimation when they learned that I had survived eight years there. As in my favourite TV series, there is a kind of hierarchy among the prison population. But soon they got to know me for the person I am, and I got to know many of them.

As I said, it was much easier for the family to visit me at Cookham Wood as I had accumulated the right to so many visits. I had visitors almost every weekend. Paddy found it very hard, he being free and his wife, whom he knew to be innocent, still locked in prison. He could hardly speak on his visits, being choked with emotion. He had been given a flat by the council and was living there along with Anne-Marie, John and Jonathan.

I was now on the home stretch, completing the last year of my sentence. Other prisoners, even those who were doing a much shorter stretch than me, would get a period of adjustment or 'rehabilitation' to prepare them for release and the outside world. This would include being taken out shopping with an officer, weekend home visits and even a week-long home visit during the period leading up to their release. Normally they would be appointed a probation officer as well who would help them get accommodation fixed up, which makes sense. In my opinion there is no point in just opening the gates and throwing the prisoner onto the street. If he or she has nowhere to live, has not learned to reintegrate into society and so on, there is a fair chance that it will not be long before they are 'guests of Her Majesty' again. In my opinion we 'Irish terrorists,' as we were classed, were denied all that. For instance, when my husband was released in February 1984, I feel I should have been given a day or weekend home visit to coincide with when he was viewing accommodation for us to live in. After all, it was going to be my home as well. I did ask for this but it was refused. Had Paddy and I been separated or had I been alone, they would have had to let me out anyway to view and find a place to stay.

It was approaching Anne-Marie's eighteenth birthday, 7 October 1984. We had talked about having a surprise party for her and, it being near my release date, that perhaps I could get one of my expected weekend home leaves to coincide with her birthday. I had dreamed of surprising her, just appearing unannounced at some point during her party. I had no worldly goods to give her but I had hoped that for her eighteenth birthday she could have something even more precious—time; the time with her mum which she had been deprived of from the age of nine. I petitioned for a home visit. I had missed my daughter's confirmation, her sixteenth birthday, her starting work; so many milestones in her young life. I thought they would grant me this home leave for her eighteenth birthday; they didn't.

Instead, they allowed the officer who went out shopping to buy me a bunch of flowers which I could give to Anne-Marie when she came to visit.

One evening, a week later, I was told not to put on my apron for my work in the kitchen the next morning because I was being taken on a shopping trip. I thought it was a joke and told the officer to stop pulling my leg. After all, they had just refused me permission to attend my youngest child's eighteenth birthday. But it wasn't a joke. The next morning I was taken to the nearest town to go shopping with an officer. It had been a taste of the freedom that awaited me and I returned to my cell that evening almost singing, 'The end of a perfect day'!

Just as I reached my cell I was called to the governor's office. My father was critically ill, I was told. There would be a taxi coming at six o'clock the next morning to take me to Gatwick. I was going to Belfast and had to give an assurance that while there I would not speak to the press or give any interviews. I was not to tell any other prisoner. My head was spinning. They had just refused me permission to go to London for the weekend and here they were sending me to Belfast. How would I get there? They would give me money for the plane ticket the next morning. But how would I get to my father's house? My sister Mary had been informed, on condition that she told no one. How ill was Daddy? He was not exactly at death's door but they thought it better that I go to see him now. Why?

The next morning, a Thursday, I was all ready with my little holdall packed. They told me I had until the Monday evening, but did explain to me that if I thought Daddy was going downhill rapidly, I could phone them and contact the local police who would have it verified by doctor's report. I promised them that, barring the worst, I would be back in my cell on Monday evening.

It was all so strange. I couldn't be trusted to visit my daughter in London a week previously and now there I was being sent over to Belfast. Surely, if I had wanted to, I could have just disappeared over the border into the Irish Republic? Was it, perhaps, that after what had happened to Giuseppe Conlon, they didn't want it on their consciences for my father to die without my having seen him?

An officer accompanied me out to the prison gate. There was snow falling abundantly and I asked the officer to wait a moment as I savoured it falling onto my upturned face. The tears ran down my cheeks. It was the first time I had felt that in nine years. If there was 'inclement weather' at Durham, we were not allowed outside but sent instead to the dreaded 'blue room.'

When we reached the gate there was a car and driver waiting. He said, 'Hello, Anne. How are you this morning?' Who was this man and how did he know my name? He was supposed to be a taxicab driver. I was not at ease. I didn't understand what was happening to me here at all. I sat in the front seat and we set off, having to go slower than normal because of the falling snow. I drank in the scenery, the fields, the animals, the trees. The driver explained that his wife was a friend of one of the officers, which was why he normally did the 'prison runs,' taking girls to the railway station usually, and that he had heard all about me. I said I supposed he had heard I was a terrible terrorist. His reply was: 'You'd be surprised who believes in your innocence.'

He came into the airport with me as I bought my ticket. The ticket clerk knew who I was. 'So they have been alerted; they know I'm coming,' were thoughts racing through my mind. Early morning, mid-week, the airport seemed to be quiet. I had flown only once before, for Mummy's funeral. Other times going back and forth to Belfast I had always had the children with me and travelled by boat. The driver couldn't accompany me further than check-in, of course, and from there I was pointed in the direction of a seating area to await embarkation of the plane. I have to admit I was disorientated, confused and frightened. Everything had happened so quickly. Were they sending me back to Belfast so that someone could assassinate me, 'wipe me out' as they say? The whole thing had an air of unreality.

As I sat in the waiting area, I was too afraid to move. I didn't buy a coffee, a newspaper, a book, nothing; I just sat there clutching my holdall and my ticket. I didn't want to move around or go to the coffee bar or into the newsagent's in case someone recognized me. In the eyes of the world I was still a guilty terrorist, tried and convicted by the highest court in the land. I would try to calm myself, 'But how would people know my face?' With my poor eyesight I tried to read the destinations and times on the distant screen, but couldn't really make them out. There was a policeman walking up and down nearby. In hindsight, he probably noticed me sitting alone and peering in an attempt to make out the flight information. But as I noticed him pacing back and forth I thought, 'He knows it's me. He's keeping an eye on me.' Then he came over to me—and asked me which flight I was waiting for. When I told him, he informed me that I was in the wrong waiting area and showed me to the correct place—just in time, as the flight was boarding.

There were hardly a dozen passengers on the flight. After take-off a stewardess asked me by name if I would like breakfast. Looking back on it now, it was probably silly of me but I felt so conspicuous that I thought they all knew who I was, they too must have known I was coming. How long had this all been arranged? They gave me breakfast, and for about ten minutes I actually debated with myself whether I should eat it. Perhaps someone had put something in it? Today I laugh when I think of it, but at the time it was not funny. The whole situation was so strange that I couldn't understand it. I prayed Jesus to let me get to Belfast: 'Just let me see Mary and Hugh and I'll know I'm safe.' As the plane came down into Belfast the tears once again rolled down my cheeks. In what strange circumstances, though, was I coming home. I had dreamed of coming back to see my father again—but in a few months' time with my husband and family when I would be once more a free woman.

Even as we got off the plane and were bused over to the terminal, I kept my eyes straight ahead. I still thought I was being tailed, kept under surveillance, that anything could happen. But inside I saw Mary and Hugh who ran straight towards me and threw their arms around me. True to their word, they had told no one I was coming. They were nervous too and Hugh said we should get out of there and into the car in case anyone recognized me. They took me first to their house, giving their sons the surprise of their life when their Aunt Anne walked in. They plied me with another big, traditional Irish breakfast which I couldn't finish. Although the food at Cookham Wood was better, the years of prison food at Durham left me with a small appetite and today I still cannot eat a big meal.

Then Hugh drove us over to my father's flat. One or two other family members were there visiting him, as there was always someone with him. There were yells and tears of joy mixed with disbelief as I walked through the door. They thought I must have been released from prison, but I told them I had to go back. Poor Daddy, of course, heard the commotion and was trying to sit up in his bed. He was ill. He was very breathless and tried to say my name, but no sound came out. Neither of us could speak. I just threw myself beside him on that bed and we cried our hearts out for a good half-hour. I held him in my arms; the poor man was reduced to skin and bone. Eventually we managed to compose ourselves a little and I spent the rest of the day there. It was all very well the Home Office saying I mustn't tell anyone I was in Belfast, but, as normal, people were popping in and out of the house all day to see how Daddy was and the news soon spread that Annie Maguire was home. But the people were good and no one contacted the media; at least not while I was there. It was published in the press later, I heard, that I had been home for the weekend.

The time passed all too quickly and many people pressed me to stay a few more days. But I had given my word. The doctor told me Daddy was very ill, but he could survive for up to another six months. Therefore, I was not going to let the authorities think I would take advantage of their letting me out for the weekend. I was back in my cell on the Monday evening.

In November of that year I was given my one and only weekend home leave before my release. That was hard. First of all, the accommodation Paddy had been given was in a block of flats. Now I knew I couldn't complain, lots of people were worse off than we were as regards accommodation, but I couldn't help thinking it was so like prison every time I had to climb those flights of stairs to reach our flat. And then, I had been used to living in a house before we were arrested, and we had always had our little garden. With what pride I had built up our little house on Third Avenue, furnishing and decorating it as best we could. Now here were my husband and son and daughter living in a little flat with bits of second-hand furniture. Anne-Marie had done her best and bought what curtains they could afford. But we did not even have a change of bedlinen, whereas before I had always kept a well-stocked linen cupboard, with plenty of towels and sheets. We would have to make our new home from naught, at our age. I was almost fifty, Paddy fifty-three.

FOURTEEN

The 22nd day of February 1985 was the long-awaited day of my release from prison. The day before, I worked like fury in our woodwork class to finish a little stool I was making for my grandson. That night I sat up to finish a pair of gloves I was knitting for an officer's son. In the morning I was sitting in my cell waiting for them to come and let me out. I had my little holdall packed. The rest of my clothes had already been sent out when the family came to visit. I had distributed the things I'd had in my cell among the other prisoners. Normally prisoners were released before eight o'clock in the morning. At nine o'clock I was still sitting there.

An officer came and told me that there was a television crew waiting outside the gates. I thought she was playing a joke on me at first but she wasn't, and she told me the authorities were trying to avoid them seeing me. There were two other prisoners being released that morning and they had sent them out in a taxi, telling them to keep their heads down in the back of the car in the hope that the film crew would think it was me!

The officer who worked in the kitchen and whom I got on well with, brought me a breakfast tray decorated with a flower and a 'Good Luck' card. Another officer told me it was unknown for that person to do this. A little after nine, the first officer returned and I insisted that I wanted out and did not want to wait any longer. After all, this was the day I had waited nine years for. I think a recurring dream I have was sparked by my wait that morning. Every so often I have a dream that I am still in prison; my release date has arrived and they are not letting me out. So I go and plead with the chief to please, please let me out.

Eventually they came and took me to reception to collect my belongings. I didn't have much and would leave prison carrying only my holdall and the little wooden stool. I knew Paddy would be waiting for me at the gates, but I wasn't expecting Vincent to be there as well, and certainly not a TV crew. I had said I wanted to come out quietly, with no fuss and no parties. But the film crew had a car waiting for us and took us to our flat in London, interviewing us as we went.

They were from RTE, the Irish state broadcasting company, and had arranged a big meeting, a sort of press conference, in a London hotel for that afternoon. That was where I first met the writer and journalist Robert Kee, who has done so much to highlight the miscarriage of justice in our case and others.

That night we just delighted in being together again as a family on the outside, all free at last. We chatted for hours, but more than anything I was completely taken with my grandson Jonathan. Of course I had seen him briefly on visits, but now I could hold and cuddle him to my heart's content. At the same time, I couldn't fight the sadness, though I tried to hide it, at the realization that when I was first locked away, Anne-Marie was only two years older than Jonathan was now. My four children were all adults, used to being independent and leading their own lives.

The next day Paddy and I were flown to Dublin to do further interviews with RTE. As we were about to board the plane the stewardess told us to wait back a moment while she 'sorted us out.' She put us in first class and served us champagne during the flight! We did interviews all day and again the next morning. When we were finished I decided to take the opportunity to go to Belfast to see Daddy and all the family since we were so near. The TV company asked if they could come along as well which, after checking by telephone with my sister Mary, we agreed to. When we arrived there, Daddy had made a superhuman effort to get out of bed and dressed, the first time in months. He was actually standing at the door to welcome me home. I was so overcome that I couldn't speak for a long time, only cry my eyes out. Here was someone else who had suffered through our wrongful conviction. He had seen his daughter, son, son-in-law and grandsons imprisoned for something they never did. Daddy, fighting for every breath, made a little speech for the camera saying how proud he was to welcome home his daughter, an innocent woman, and appealing to the Government to act to clear our names.

As he spoke so valiantly, I cried and cried. People reading this and those who saw the documentary may think me a terrible 'cry-baby,' but I could see that my father didn't have long to live. It was costing him much to be out of bed and speaking those few words. He had told a cousin of his who is a priest that he would live to see me a free woman once again. He did just that. Within a fortnight, though, he was dead. I really thought my heart would break at the time—we had had so little time together—yet I can console myself with the knowledge that at least he did live to see me free, as he said he would. I would love to have had the time to speak to him a bit about our experience, to tell him about how good and kind some people were in prison—Chief Clough, Joanie Barr and others.

Back home in London, media interest continued to grow apace. Paddy and I did a television programme with Robert Kee for Channel Four, and were interviewed by David Frost on 'Good Morning, Britain,' both of which were transmitted in the April. Goodwill messages and letters flooded in. In order to respond to all of them, we eventually had to print up a standard response from Paddy on behalf of the whole family.

As we had lost all our possessions while we were in prison, with the house being flooded and John being moved into a smaller flat, we had to start trying to build up a home again. Pam and Joe Hoey who had the local pub offered me a cleaning job for which I will ever be grateful as it helped restore my confidence. I couldn't have borne to go around seeking work and being turned down because I was a convicted criminal.

As a result of people reading about our case, and those television programmes, I began to be recognized wherever I went, which is something I live with to this day. On the whole, people just want to come up and wish you well and ask how you are coping now. It can sometimes be tiring but I do appreciate people's concern and goodwill and their desire to express it. Where possible I prefer just to listen while quietly asking God to bless the person for their goodness. One thing I never do is get involved in any discussion about politics.

In those first months after my release I did press, radio and television interviews in Belfast and Dublin. Once when I was in Dublin Airport to begin a homeward journey, I popped in to buy a bottle of wine to bring back as a gift to someone. As I don't know anything about wine, I asked the manager to advise me on a good buy. When he wrapped it for me he also gave me a bottle of champagne. He said he knew who I was from the television programmes and asked me to keep that bottle of champagne to pop the day our innocence would be proved and we did! News reports after our convictions were quashed in 1992 showed us opening that long-guarded bottle of champagne. People have been very kind as our story and the extent of the miscarriage of justice we suffered has become better known. I'm almost always recognized when I fly over to Belfast to visit my relatives, and airport staff greet me with a 'Nice to see you back again, Mrs Maguire.'

In May of 1985, Channel Four broadcast a shorter version of the RTE documentary. Four days later the former MP Gerry Fitt, who was by then Lord Fitt, initiated a debate on our case in the House of Lords. He raised the whole question of the unreliability of the TLC forensic test which had formed the basis for our conviction, and the Government Minister, Lord Glenarthur, stated that now there must be corroboration of forensic tests before a case can be brought to court. The Home Secretary, however, still refused to review our case.

Shortly after my release I went with my husband, and our two sons who had been imprisoned, to see our constituency MP, John Wheeler. I asked him, if he had the time, to listen to our story; to accept me, Anne Maguire, as he found me before him and to forget for the moment about the press reports of 'Evil Aunt Annie.' He did listen courteously and when I had finished stood up and shook my hand. He said he had heard Sir John Biggs-Davison (since deceased) speak about our case and, now that he had met me as his constituent and heard our story, he would do all in his power to clear our name. I will always be grateful to him for listening to me that day and for keeping his promise. He did speak about us in Parliament.

A campaign started to clear the names of 'The Maguire Seven' and to obtain the release of the wrongly-convicted 'Guildford Four' who were still serving their sentences. We were invited to join in with the campaign for 'The Birmingham Six' but thought at the time that we should combine ours with that for the Guildford Four, as the cases were so linked; a decision I have since regretted.

Meetings were held around the country to highlight our cause, give out information and answer questions. Money was raised and the campaign was even taken to America. But, it must be stated clearly, neither I nor any of my family received any money from those funds. The people who went to speak in the USA were people who had never spent a night in a cell themselves. The only money ever used by me was when an office-bearer of the campaign bought a train ticket for me to go on a speaking tour of the north of England. On that occasion Lisa Astin, Carole Richardson's friend who had been with her at a pop concert the night the Guildford bombs went off, came with me to represent Carole, who was still in prison. We were put up by a Church of England vicar and his wife, who became good friends thereafter.

Public figures also campaigned to have the Guildford and Maguire cases reopened and re-examined; among them Sir John Biggs-Davison MP, Christopher Price MP, Lord Fitt who had been MP for West Belfast, former Home Secretaries Roy Jenkins and Merlyn Rees, Law Lords Devlin and Scarman.

I believe a turning point came in the perception of both the public and officialdom when, above all others,

Cardinal Basil Hume, the Archbishop of Westminster, decided to speak out. People, from the highest ranks of government to the man in the street, knew that he did not lightly pronounce on matters such as this. And although certain church figures, such as Sister Sarah and others, had stood by me, they had no public voice or strong influence. The senior Catholic churchman in England and Wales did, though. In 1986 he wrote a letter to *The Times*. In 1987 he appeared in a 'First Tuesday' TV programme and led a delegation to see the then Home Secretary, Douglas Hurd.

The Cardinal had visited Giuseppe Conlon in prison and obviously saw that as well as being a sick man, Giuseppe was a gentle person who wouldn't hurt a fly. When Giuseppe died still protesting his and our innocence, it left an impression on the Cardinal. In fact, I cannot speak highly enough of him. He has done so much to help and encourage me and all my family that we hold him not only in great respect but also in love and affection.

In 1989 the verdicts on the Guildford Four were quashed and they were released. Shortly afterwards, just by chance, I bumped into Carole Richardson and her friend (who became her sister-in-law) in the street, actually crossing the road. As we threw our arms around each other and laughed and wept for joy right there in the middle of the road, I think we practically caused a traffic jam! We went for a coffee and agreed that Carole would come to visit me once she had settled into her new life of freedom.

A couple of weeks later I received a phone call from Archbishop's House. The Cardinal would soon be making a parish visitation in our area and would we mind if he called in to see us? Would we mind? We were overjoyed!

The day of the expected visit arrived and I had cleaned and double-cleaned our little flat. We were all there waiting for our important visitor to arrive when the doorbell rang. Just by chance—now I prefer to call it Providence—it was Carole Richardson and her friend Lisa Astin. I welcomed them and told them they might not believe the coincidence, but we were just expecting the Cardinal to arrive at any moment. They protested that they would call another time but, of course, I would have none of that. My home was always open to friends, and it would remain so even if a Cardinal was calling. Carole spurned the offer of a chair and, just as she had always done in prison, plonked herself down on the floor. She had become a Catholic in prison, so I was happy that now she would have the chance to meet our Archbishop in person.

When the Cardinal arrived I welcomed him in similar fashion, telling him he wouldn't believe this but Carole and Lisa had just arrived on a surprise visit. He was delighted and we all sat and had tea, chatting away for a couple of hours. He knew that since my release I had gone on a pilgrimage to the French Marian shrine of Lourdes with my sister Mary, and asked me how I had found it. I was full of praise for the beauty of the place and the peace of heart I had experienced there. The Cardinal then asked if I would like to return there on a pilgrimage he would be leading, and if Carole and Lisa would like to come as well. He told Carole he would like to show her the exact spot where he heard that she had been freed.

That October we did all go to Lourdes with the pilgrimage from Westminster Diocese, led by His Eminence. He did take us to the exact spot on the meadow opposite the grotto shrine where he had been praying the psalms when a young priest had come running to tell him the news that the Guildford Four had been freed. It was a moving moment and we all knelt down as the Cardinal led us in a prayer of thanksgiving. My son Patrick has since then also gone on a pilgrimage of young people to Lourdes, led by the Cardinal. Afterwards he published an article in a Catholic newspaper recounting the effect it had on him.

Now I have been to Lourdes three times in all. Despite what many people say about the commercialism of the town, once you are off the town's streets and enter into the sanctuary domaine itself, it is a place of great prayer and peace. As I called on the prayers of the Blessed Virgin all through my prison sentence, I always feel as if I am arriving at her door and saying, 'Hey it's me, Anne. I'm home; you got me through it.'

With my sister Mary, I have also been to a pilgrimage site in the former Yugoslavia, the little village of Medjugorje, where six young people claim that the Virgin Mary has been appearing daily since 1980. When I was in jail, to keep my spirits up, Mary and I would often plan the pilgrimages we would make when I would be free. If I go abroad now, it has to be somewhere special like that, somewhere with a message of peace and hope attached, a 'holy place.' I have no ambitions to travel, but if we do go somewhere again, I would like it to be Rome or even the Holy Land where Our Lord walked on earth. In our world of today, with so much turmoil and so many innocent victims of wars, famine and injustice, we need to work and pray for peace and justice for all.

FIFTEEN

In October 1989 the Government appointed former Appeals Court Judge, Sir John May, to lead an investigation into the convictions of the Maguire Seven. He conducted a thorough investigation into our prosecution and trial, and held public hearings. On 12 July 1990 he produced an 'interim report.' That very same day the Home Secretary referred our case to the Court of Appeal again.

It's worth quoting the reasons Sir John gave for such a move to be necessary. He concluded that:

1) 'the Crown could no longer be taken to have proved' that there were traces of nitro-glycerine on our hands and my plastic gloves;
2) the whole 'scientific basis' upon which our prosecution was based had been so discredited that 'on this basis alone the Court of Appeal should be invited to set aside the convictions;'
3) there were serious errors in the conduct of our trial;
4) the 'possibility of innocent contamination' of our hands and my gloves had not been excluded at the trial.

Our appeal was held from 7 May to 10 June 1991. Pat O'Neil and my brother Sean came over from Ireland. In truth, as at the trial, there was a lot of legal and scientific jargon and it wasn't always easy to follow what was being said. On the last day of all of this we still didn't have a result. The three judges had to go away and consider their verdict. Finally, on 26 June, the result was announced and our convictions in 1976 of having handled explosives were quashed.

The crowds of wellwishers outside the court were so great that the police had to clear a way through for us. I was so overwhelmed by all these people pressing in on us, wanting to congratulate us, that I just followed as my brother Sean led me by the hand through the throng to a waiting car. I couldn't hope to acknowledge or speak to them all, but I am truly grateful to all those kind people who turned up at the courthouse to express their goodwill.

That day we opened the bottle of champagne as I had promised the kind shopkeeper at Dublin airport who had given it to me six years previously. At last, fifteen years after we had all been sent to prison for a crime we never committed, the highest appeal court in the land recognized that we had been wrongly convicted.

And yet, the reason they chose to give for that quashing was the possibility that we may have been 'innocently contaminated.' It was as if they still wanted to maintain the reliability of the discredited TLC test. The scientific committee set up by Sir John could have carried out an investigation into the unique pattern of the test results obtained in 1974. They were unwilling to do so. Two independent scientists—Dr Lloyd representing the Conlon family and Dr Caddy representing us—showed that the pattern of results of those TLC tests in 1974 could only be explained as a result of laboratory contamination of ether, which was used to extract the swabs of our hands. Sir John did not accept that this was the explanation. He only conceded that it was a possibility. We were disappointed because that could still leave room for doubt and, as we feared, it has allowed a 'whispering campaign' where some people still say 'Oh yes, they've been found innocent after all, but no smoke without fire; how could they have been "innocently contaminated" with nitro-glycerine?'

And so we still have a certain cloud of doubt hanging over us all the time in the minds of some people. This is hard to bear. That day when our convictions were overturned I said to the others, 'I don't know about you, but I cannot let this rest like this. I am going to fight on. This result leaves open the possibility that we were all somehow 'innocently contaminated,' from a towel for instance, and I know—as you do—that there was never anything like that in my house.' They all agreed wholeheartedly, so I and they continue to speak out on the truth of our case until this day.

In December 1992, Sir John May produced his final report on our case and the others connected with the bomb attacks on Guildford and Woolwich. It did not receive much public attention as it was overshadowed by another horrific IRA bomb attack, on the English town of Warrington, which killed two young children.

In that document he summarized the four reasons he had given in his previous report as to why our convictions should not be allowed to stand. He barely concealed his disappointment that our appeal had taken so long to come to court—almost a year after he had made his recommendation, on 12 July 1990. And he made no secret of the general astonishment that the Court of Appeal 'clearly found itself unable to agree with any of the other conclusions to which I had come in my interim report. Understandably, the judgement of the Court was not well received, either by the Maguire Seven or by the many who had been campaigning on their behalf.'

In a television interview he said that ours was the worst miscarriage of justice he had ever seen. His report also recommended setting up an independent body to investigate other alleged miscarriages of justice. This was later endorsed by a Royal Commission on Criminal Justice which made the same recommendation.

Sir John's investigation was delayed by the trial in 1993 of three detectives who had been involved in the investigation of the Guildford bombing. It was not an easy time for us as we were once more the subject of public discussion. Sometimes it felt as though we were being tried again, at least in the public's minds. Whether we will ever be free of the stigma of having been convicted, even though wrongly, we will always bear the scars of what has happened to us.

One day I was in a taxi with two children coming from school. That day there was a visiting head of state arriving in London. Of course there were a lot of police vehicles on the road to clear the path for his motorcade. At one point two police motor cycles became positioned in front of our car and two behind. For any other citizen that wouldn't cause any problem, if anything a bit of excitement perhaps. For me, though, it revived memories, and all the feelings associated with them, of the time I was being transferred to Durham jail to begin my sentence, and of the time I was being taken out of prison to be operated on in Newcastle. It shouldn't but it did. You see, we can never really be a 'normal' family again. We have to live and cope with what happened as best we can, and we do that by mutual love and support.

It was not easy coming out of prison and getting back together again with my husband. Of course we both still loved each other, and still do, but we were two different people after our ten years apart and all our different experiences. We had to take the time to get to know one another again as the persons we had become. Paddy, as he always has done, prefers to live a very quiet life. He has good days and bad days, as we all do, remembering and trying to cope with all that has happened to us. He likes to stay at his own fireside, which is why he hasn't accompanied me on my pilgrimages with Mary, although he is happy for me to go. His main concern, as it has always been, is for his wife and family. I shall always be grateful to Paddy for the love we have shared which has given us such a beautiful family. The children (and now their children) hold him in the greatest love and respect.

My sons have all suffered broken relationships, and people tell me that would probably have happened anyway as it is such a common problem today. I don't know. It can't be easy for any young woman to come into our family, which is so tremendously close, and to understand the hurts we all feel at different times and the need we have to be near each other. Since Anne-Marie shyly told me during a visit when I was in Cookham Wood that she had a boyfriend, she and Terry have been together and have a beautiful little daughter.

We all live within walking distance of each other in West London. Everything I do, I do with my family in mind. Thus, when we received an initial payment of our eventual compensation, I put a deposit on a little maisonette near the flat where Paddy and I have lived since our release. I have been fortunate to find a job to keep up the payments, while we await news of a final decision regarding compensation. Eight years since my release after serving a sentence for a wrongful conviction, we are still waiting to hear what the final decision will be on that matter. If it is not given us, I shall have to give up the house. But for the moment we are grateful for each day we can be together. The family members drop in individually and I love to hear and see what the grandchildren have been doing at school that day, what books they are reading now. Sunday lunch is our gathering point when we all spend the afternoon together until it's time for the grandchildren to go home and prepare for school again the next day.

I still have the little photo of Anne-Marie in her school uniform which hung in my cell. Now her daughter is the same age as she was when we were arrested. The first time we went shopping in a supermarket after my release, I asked Anne-Marie if she would like a bar of chocolate. When she said, 'No thanks, Mum, I'll just go and get some cigarettes,' it struck home to me that she was no longer my little girl but a grown-up young woman. Since we missed those growing-up years, particularly with the youngest two, Anne-Marie and Patrick, Paddy and I are determined we won't miss any of it in their children, our grandchildren. Patrick is very strongly affected by the news or sight of other victims of violence or injustice, particularly when they are children. He has written in newspapers. When Mrs McKeowen in Dublin started a peace movement after the deaths of two little children in the Warrington bombings, she was on the Jimmy Young radio show one day. She was telling him about the peace rally she had organized in Dublin for that evening. Moved by her response, Patrick telephoned the radio show to encourage her. Several other listeners telephoned the Jimmy Young show saying they were touched by Patrick's call, and as a result he was flown to Dublin, courtesy of an anonymous listener, to address the rally that very evening.

He and I have spoken at various peace rallies and meetings. We too were victims of the IRA and of a miscarriage of justice, therefore if we can help anyone in similar circumstances or draw attention to their plight, it's the least we can do.

In the summer of 1993, Anne-Marie and I were interviewed together on Britain's Channel Four by Mavis Nicholson. It is painful to go over our hurts and experiences in public, but we felt that if it could illustrate what happened to us by being falsely implicated in a crime we never committed and, above all, if we could offer some hope to those separated from loved ones by whatever circumstances forced upon them, then it was worth doing.

On Boxing Day 1993 a new film was premièred in Ireland. It was called *In the Name of the Father* and reportedly told the story of Gerard Conlon and his developing relationship with his father Giuseppe up until Giuseppe's death in London while still a prisoner.

We had heard reports that such a film was being made, but at no time were we approached by the makers. Our lawyer had obtained a copy of the script and said some of the ways in which I and my family were portrayed were 'deeply offensive.' Some amendments were made to the film but, unfortunately, other inaccuracies concerning us remained. Of course, once it had opened in Ireland, both in the Republic and in the North, we began to get reports of what was actually in the final version of the film, and people who knew us and our story began to express their grave misgivings. The film was scheduled to open in England in early February with much attendant publicity. It was arranged for myself, Paddy and the family, along with Carole Richardson and our lawyer and faithful friend Alastair Logan, to see the film privately and meet with the director before it opened to the public.

I must say that I was delighted when I heard such a film was being made. I am all for anything that will spread the truth about our cases—the Guildford Four and the Maguire Seven—and I was especially happy that Giuseppe would be honoured in such a fashion. Alas, when we did see the film, we were aghast. We were totally unprepared for the inaccuracies and the amount of 'artistic licence' taken. The portrayal of me and members of my family was unrecognizable. In fact, when the actress playing me made her first appearance on screen, Carole had to tell me it was supposed to be me.

This scene showed me serving breakfast in my house to Gerard Conlon and Paul Hill. As I have already written, and repeated ever since the evening I was arrested in 1974, Paul Hill was never in my house. And Gerard had certainly not been in my house at any time since I had barred him from coming to it after what he had done to us the previous time we had taken him in. When he left Belfast for London at the time portrayed in the film, he was heading to his Uncle Hugh and Aunt Kitty Maguire's house, not mine. The film showed him bringing me sausages sent by his mother in Belfast. I explained to the film's director, Jim Sheridan, that I only ever saw Sarah Conlon whenever I visited their house to see Paddy's mother. As I had no relationship with Sarah, it was therefore misleading to portray her sending something to me from Belfast. As the controversy grew surrounding the film in its opening week, Mr Sheridan made an outburst on a Radio Four arts programme about 'Annie Maguire and her bloody sausages,' thus trivializing the whole thing. I'm afraid some people hearing him may have thought I was only concerned with petty details. It was not so.

We finally issued a statement to the press. It read as follows:

Statement by Patrick and Anne Maguire and family

We have been subjected to considerable pressure from the Media to respond to the film *In the Name of the Father*. We have only very recently been able to see the film. We were not consulted about the making of the film by the makers of the film because they were told by Gerard Conlan that we would be hostile to it. We would never hinder anyone who wished to make an honest and truthful account of our case. There is no feud between our family and the Conlon family. We believe that the assertion that there is a feud is a publicity tactic employed by those who wish to attack the film.

We are impressed by the artistic merits of the film which dramatically depicts parts of the history of the miscarriages of justice in our case and that of the Guildford Four. We are concerned with the accuracy of a film in depicting events with which we were connected. Our concerns have been characterized as 'sour grapes' because this was not a film about our family. We have never solicited such a film. All we have ever asked of anyone is that they tell the truth. When we see untruths about us and our case we correct them. We have been doing so since 1974. If in seeking to ensure that the truth is told about us and the miscarriage of justice in our case we are perceived to be acting contrary to the 'spirit' in which the film is made then we have no apology to make.

We understand that the makers of this film assert that the film is 'faction,' meaning a mixture of fact and fiction. Only those who have a knowledge of these cases would know what is fact and what is fiction. In the absence of any qualification by the makers the viewer may assume that this film is a documentary account. Documentaries represent real events. The film's audience may leave the cinema believing that what they saw is fact. Much of the detail in this film is fiction.

Our trial is depicted as having taken place jointly with the Guildford Four and the film conveys the impression that we were tried jointly on the same enterprise. That is completely untrue. Also untrue is the depiction in the film of Paul Hill and Gerard Conlon eating a meal at our house on their arrival in England. Anne Maguire met Gerard Conlon and Paul Hill in October 1974, some two weeks after the Guildford Bombings had occurred, at a public social function. That was the first and only time she had met Paul Hill before her arrest. None of the other members of our family had ever met him before his arrest. Gerard Conlon had stayed at our house previously when he had been in England in 1973 but was no longer welcome there, as he knew in 1974, because of his behaviour. We therefore had no idea that Gerard was in this country in 1974 until Anne saw him at the function.

The suggestion that Gerard Conlon signed a blank statement form into which Anne's name was put by the police is also untrue. He made two long statements both of which were written by himself. Moreover, the Conlon family never sent any food parcels to us.

The case against us was factually and evidentially completely different from that of the Guildford Four. Mrs Peirce did not become involved until 1988, eight years after Giuseppe's death, when she commenced representing Gerard Conlon. We do not owe the quashing of the convictions to her.

The evidence of police perjury and fabrication which secured the quashing of the convictions of the Guildford Four, and thus the re-examination of our case, was found by the Avon and Somerset Police in the papers of the Surrey Police. The evidence which secured the quashing of our convictions was discovered during and after Sir John May's enquiry. Our debt of gratitude is owed to a large number of people for their belief in us and for their support and hard work over many years to achieve justice in our case and that of the Guildford Four. People like Robert Kee, Yorkshire Television, Ros Franey, Grant McKee, Cardinal Basil Hume and his Deputation, Sir John May and his enquiry team and those in the Police Service and the media who were prepared to look for the truth beyond the lies and the prejudice. None of these are mentioned in the film. Nor are the victims of the bombings.

This film is a dramatic interpretation of events and should not be regarded as a factual account of them. We are concerned to ensure that the truth about us and our case is not allowed to become a casualty. We regard the truth as our defence against those who would seek to malign us. We have always told the truth and we will continue to do so.

After our private viewing of the film, I told Mr Sheridan I would have been happy to help him in any way if he had only approached us. My son Patrick was beside me as we spoke and Mr Sheridan started to explain that it was all a matter of limited resources and there being only so much money available in making a film. In unison, Patrick and I said 'Hold on there a minute.' We were stunned that he should think we would have been looking for payment and I told him we would have been only too happy to help in any way we could with a film which would tell the truth and honour Giuseppe. After some discussion, Patrick told the director, 'You made a good job of making the film *My Left Foot*, but I'm afraid it looks as if you did this one with your left foot.' Sheridan had to laugh.

At another pre-première showing, held in the Houses of Parliament on 1 February 1994, a journalist asked Mr Sheridan in front of all the MPs and Lords who had gathered to see the film if he would publicly make it clear that the film was not in fact 'a true story,' not a documentary-style presentation of the facts? He congratulated him on the artistic merits of the film as it stood, but said he was concerned that, if the viewing public took it to be a true story, then it messed around with the integrity of 'characters' in the film—who were in fact living characters, people like the Maguire family and Carole Richardson. Mr Sheridan never replied.

Shortly before the film opened in London, the *Sunday Times* ran a story about the film and its inaccuracies. I did not want any acrimony and was afraid that people might think I was trying to undermine the film, or, as some media reports suggested at first, that it was somehow a case of 'sour grapes' because the film was not based on our story. Nothing could be further from the truth. And that was my only concern. Besides, what these critics did not know was that an international television company had just finished filming a documentary about me and our case which will be shown in dozens of countries around the world.

The story grew and grew and, apart from the details of our case and the injustice of portraying us in situations that in reality we had never been in, it certainly sparked a debate in the British press and media. There was much discussion about the role of such films and where the line should be drawn between straight presentation of the facts and how much 'artistic licence' should be afforded film makers in such cases. Some described it as the question of 'faction,' that is the mixing of fact and fiction, and arts and media critics lined up on one side or the other. In June 1994, four months after the film opened in London, I saw a report in British newspapers that Britain's Advertising Standards Authority condemned the film's distributors for saying on initial publicity posters that the film was a 'true story.' In fairness to them, I must point out that they later changed the posters to read 'based on a true story.' I don't know who made the complaint to the Advertising Standards Authority—the newspaper report just said that it was brought by a 'member of the public'—but it does justify the concerns our family and so many members of the public had about representing fictional elements as fact.

Although I did not speak out when all the reporters were clamouring for a comment around the time of the film's opening, I did answer directly and simply when asked my opinion during television and radio interviews when my book was published a few weeks later in Ireland and Britain.

Also, I did not, and do not want to get involved in any sort of police-bashing or British Government-bashing. What was done to us was wrong. People made mistakes and I will simply tell the truth about what happened to us. When this book was published in Britain, one interviewer told me I should continually 'name names.' He meant I should keep exposing the names of individual people who were bad to us or mistreated us.

As I replied to him, those people know who they are. They don't need me to keep reminding them. They have their own consciences and they must reconcile themselves to their past, to the mistakes which were made, and to their God. I prefer to work to a positive end, and not enter into negative recriminations. The history of my home city, Belfast, is surely enough proof that such a road leads nowhere.

CHAPTER
SIXTEEN

With all the controversy that arose over the film in February 1994, I was practically under telephone siege from the media wanting comment. I decided, though, to leave it to our family lawyer Alastair Logan. Just after that, near the end of the month, he and I flew to Canada together, along with my sister Mary. We had been invited to address a congress there, organized by The Association in Defence of the Wrongly Convicted, dealing with all sorts of miscarriages of justice.

Mary and I were guests of a lovely couple, Lisa and Karl Pomerant and their children, who treated us as if we were part of their own family. I was privileged to meet Rubin 'Hurricane' Carter, Subway Elvis and others. They suffered terribly from miscarriages of justice and my heart went out to them and their families.

Fortunately that trip coincided with a holiday period at my work. A week later my employers kindly gave me leave when this book was launched in the United Kingdom and Ireland on 8 March. I was whisked off on a round of interviews all over England and in Dublin and Belfast. Friends and neighbours joked that it must be wonderful leading a glamorous life going from one TV or radio studio to another. Far from it! It was completely exhausting. I have nothing but admiration for all those actors, pop stars and others who do it all the time—and still appear fresh and bubbly.

The first interview was on the number one TV chat show in Ireland, 'The Late Late Show,' compèred by Gay Byrne. I was rather nervous at first, as it's reckoned that at least one person in every household in the country tunes into this Friday night show, and it was done in front of a studio audience. After a few minutes, though, Gay soon put me at ease and I felt a bit more relaxed. My sister Mary and her husband had driven down from Belfast to spend the night with me, and what a night it turned out to be! Dublin was hosting an international rugby match the next day between the home team and the Scottish team. Every hotel in town was packed full with enthusiastic supporters of the two teams. It would be difficult to say who likes their celebratory drink the more—the Irish with their Guinness and 'Irish,' or the Scots with their Export and Scotch! But everyone was in good humour and there was a great atmosphere in the city.

The captain and two players of the Irish side were fellow guests on the chat show that evening and it was a real pleasure to meet them. They were true gentlemen and a credit to their country. Luckily for them, they also won on their home turf the next day!

Exactly a week later my tour ended with me crossing the Irish Sea once more to return to my home town of Belfast. There I was a guest on Ulster Television's 'Kelly Show' and afterwards we had a lovely party with all my family and other guests on the show. My trip back to London on the Sunday evening brought with it a reminder that the 'Troubles' are far from over. That evening the IRA launched a rocket attack on a runway at Heathrow Airport. One terminal was closed and all the passengers were squeezed into the terminal I landed at.

163

It took me four hours to get out of the place. I returned to work the next morning tired, grateful for the opportunity I had had to put over the truth about the Maguire Seven, but also happy to go back to being a housewife and ordinary worker and not a media personality.

I need to keep up my little job to get by. As I earn only a basic wage, I have to 'sign on' every two weeks with the Department of Employment to keep up my National Insurance credits for an eventual retirement pension. In turn, once a fortnight they send me a cheque for the grand sum of twenty pence (thirty US cents). Some people say I should not work at all, in that case, and should claim unemployment benefit. But I am an independent person and I've always worked. I'm proud still to do that and in any case I need a secure income, however small. We still have not received any further compensation from the Government since one small interim payment after our convictions were quashed. We don't know when we shall be compensated. I use that official word 'compensated' but, of course, no amount of money can ever repay us for all we went through. And apart from those of us who went to jail, how could you ever compensate my two children who were left parentless on the outside? They were practically orphaned and had to grow up without their mum and dad.

My daughter Anne-Marie is expecting a second child in August 1994 and we are all delighted that she and Terry are to be parents once again and that little Lee-Anne will have a brother or sister. Patrick has a new baby son, Billy-Joe, the pride and joy of his elder brother Patrick Maguire III.

I still worry continuously about Patrick. His regular beatings by the police whenever they catch him on his own have continued. Right up until June 1993. One

Sunday night he was walking along the road returning from a social evening with some of his friends. He saw a police car stopped outside a shop whose burglar alarm was ringing. Patrick, being a very open and friendly character, stopped to chat with the two police officers attending the alarm. Just then a police van pulled up and the policemen in it jumped out and attacked Patrick. They then threw him in the van to continue their dirty work. As on previous occasions, with every kick and punch they gave him, they shouted 'that's your compensation, you bastard.'

I nearly passed out when I saw the state of Patrick on my doorstep the next morning. They had taken him in and kept him all night in the police station without even giving him his legal right to one telephone call to tell us where he was. The next day, he was finally persuaded to see a doctor. Then we received the news that the police were charging *him* with having assaulted *them*. As Patrick said, how he could have assaulted four policemen while they had him on the ground with his hands 'cuffed behind his back, was a mystery. I had a terribly worrying time until the case came to trial. It was a serious charge and if they found him guilty he could be sent to prison again. I don't think he, or I, could cope with that. In the event, the three magistrates hearing the case were not impressed by the evidence of the police and threw the case out of court, dismissing all charges. Alastair Logan, on our behalf, contacted the Police Complaints Authority and he and Patrick ended up meeting the senior police officer at our local police station. I still worry every time he goes out alone. But then, he doesn't go out much now. Since that last kicking and beating he is practically crippled with a back complaint and many days literally cannot walk. I wonder if the suffering will ever come to an end for Patrick and my other children. Patrick was deeply affected by being suddenly arrested at the age of thirteen and then thrown into prison as a terrorist. He still sees a psychiatrist to this day in his attempts to deal with it all. He is writing his own story and I hope it will be published one day. The world should know what such a miscarriage of justice can do to a child, the youngest person in Britain ever to be sent to jail for alleged terrorist offences.

My second son, John, had to fend for himself since the age of sixteen when his mum and dad were imprisoned, and today he is still independent and self-sufficient. Vincent studied and trained for two and a half years to gain the necessary certificate—'the Knowledge'—to be a registered London cab driver. It involves memorizing thousands upon thousands of streets and routes in London, Europe's largest capital, and then going before an examining board to be tested in the Knowledge. In April 1994 he finally achieved that goal and immediately leased a black London cab. He is divorced and hopes to marry his girlfriend Joyce in the fall of 1994.

Paddy, my husband, suffers from his nerves since all this happened to us. He continues to live in the council flat he was allocated when he came out of jail a year before me, in the hope of one day buying it for the family when we are eventually compensated. The two little flats are on opposite sides of the one road and there is always to-ing and fro-ing between them. He is very supportive of all the work I do to make the truth of our case known.

My brother Sean, as with so many of us in similar situations, found it hard to cope with life 'on the outside' again. His children were no longer children but independent adults. As we have all found, it takes time to build up relationships again after being separated for so many years, and Sean and his wife Teresa eventually separated.

166

Teresa died in 1991. Sean works hard at his job; he gets on well with his son and two daughters and, like me, adores his grandchildren.

Our friend Pat O'Neil, whose little girls I was looking after on that terrible night when we were all arrested, now lives a quiet life in a rural area of Ireland. His sentence had been reduced from twelve years to eight at our first appeal in 1977. When his time came to be released, he was being held in a high-security prison on the Isle of Wight, off the south coast of England. The story of his treatment, even on release, is truly a shocking one. First there was a crossing by hovercraft from the Isle of Wight to mainland England. The vessel was filled with schoolchildren on an outing. The police officers handcuffed Pat to themselves and thus he was transported, to the shock and fear of the schoolchildren, on the day of his release. That was not the end of his humiliation, though.

It had been decided to deport him, although he had lived in London since 1958. However, during Pat's imprisonment his wife moved to Ireland. She could not put up with the harassment she suffered being the wife of a 'convicted IRA terrorist.' They communicated by letter. Pat did not know the Republic of Ireland and all he had was the address of his family's new home from his wife's letters—he had never been to that village in the west of Ireland. When he and his police guards reached Heathrow, he still handcuffed to them, the pilot of the first flight to Dublin refused to take him on board. The next pilot reluctantly agreed to take him, provided the officers removed the handcuffs.

Poor Pat was a nervous wreck. Not only was he being treated as a criminal, but he had never even flown in an aeroplane before. When it landed at Dublin, some kind stranger helped him out by giving him the bus fare from the airport to the city. From there, Pat, who had no money, began to walk to that village in the west of Ireland. He had never been there. He did not know where the house was situated. He knew nothing about the place except whatever Helen had mentioned in her letters. It took him three days to arrive. And the only reason he found his wife was because he walked up to the local railway station, and there, waiting on the platform, were neighbours who had befriended his wife and daughters. Helen and they knew the date he would be released and since then had turned up at the local railway station every day expecting him off the daily train from Dublin. Like all of us, he had to face the difficulties of starting again after all that had happened to us. Sadly, under all the strain, his marriage broke down. He had the usual difficulty of getting to know his children again, which he has done. He now works as a plumber in Ireland.

Like all of us, he can never live a normal life again. We are all scarred by what happened to us. I myself still don't go into the city centre of London. There is still a danger of bombs going off there, which they do all too frequently at the moment. I am just too afraid that something would happen while I was there. I would freeze, not wanting to run for safety lest it be reported that Annie Maguire was seen running from the scene. Even in our own local area, I don't go out on my own at night. I don't mind going down to local shops in daylight or around to our local church. But I do suffer from mild panic attacks and start to get dizzy and breathless. Recently I have come near to blacking out on several occasions and now my doctor tells me I am anaemic and have low blood pressure.

Our experience has certainly taught me never to be quick to condemn others, or believe all you hear about them or read in the press. I really believe we should listen carefully to people accused of a crime or any wrongdoing, and not repeat what happened to us when we were denied the opportunity to speak out and tell our whole story.

On 30 June 1994, Sir John May published his final report on the Guildford and Woolwich bombings—this one focusing on the case of the Guildford Four. While he criticized the Surrey police and the Crown Prosecution for certain aspects of their conduct around the case, many people felt he could have been much more specific. He did, though, recommend once again that an independent body be set up to investigate alleged miscarriages of justice, taking them out of the hands of the Home Secretary.

Sir John referred to the 'confessions' beaten out of the Guildford Four: 'They contend that the confessions were in no way voluntary; that each had been induced by oppression. This, they said, had comprised assaults, threats of assaults and threats of violence against members of their families. While questioned at length they had been deprived of sleep, food and drink.'

'Having regard to the public outrage over these bombings which were followed shortly afterwards by the Birmingham pub bombings, I would not have been surprised if any police force had adopted a hostile approach; the police may have been threatening, they may even have behaved improperly; at this length of time [from the events] I am in no position to make findings on these questions.'

I found it very disturbing that a senior figure of the legal establishment should not have been surprised if the police acted aggressively and brutally, in fact taking upon themselves the role of arresting officers, judge and jury as they mistreated prisoners in their custody. If a former judge, appointed by the Government to carry out a top-level enquiry, can dismiss such behaviour as almost inevitable in the circumstances, then it is a very sad day indeed for human rights in a country which once prided itself on the rule of law and the upholding of natural justice. It used to be said that a prisoner was innocent until proved guilty. If an official Government report can make such casual references to the mistreatment of such prisoners by the police, what message does that put out?

Sir John ended his report by saying, 'It is impossible twenty years after the event to discover the truth of what happened at all points in the story. The truth, where I have not been able to establish it, must now and hereafter remain a matter for the consciences of those concerned.'

Our lawyer Alastair Logan, who also represented Patrick Armstrong and Carole Richardson of the Guildford Four, was quoted in the press the day after the report was published. He said, 'At the end of the day, four people spent 15 years in jail for an offence they didn't commit, and no-one really knows after reading that report why that happened.' He said the report took the view that it was just something that happens sometimes, and added, 'I think our criminal justice system should be proof against it.' He also regretted that the nature of Sir John's enquiry (unlike that dealing with ours, the Guildford Four enquiry was held in secret) had allowed the whispering campaign to continue.

Since this book was published in Britain, I have received letters from English people apologizing for how the legal system let us down, as if somehow it were their fault. I don't condemn anybody.

I still worry about all my children and I pray every day that they will find it in their hearts to forgive those who wrongly implicated us, wrongly convicted and sentenced us, as I do.

Above all, it is my earnest prayer that no mother, no family ever again goes through what happened to us. It is incumbent on our lawmakers and judicial experts to ensure that it doesn't—in any country. If my recounting our story and the effects which a miscarriage of justice have had on us can help that aim, then I thank God.

CHRONOLOGY

14 November 1935	I was born in Belfast.
26 September 1957	Paddy and I marry in Belfast. We set sail for London following the wedding party.
8 August 1958	Our first son, Vincent, born in London.
22 July 1959	John born in London.
24 March 1961	Patrick born in Belfast.
7 October 1966	Anne-Marie born in London.
21 September 1967	Mummy dies in Belfast.
5 October 1974	The IRA bombs two public houses in the small English town of Guildford, Surrey, killing five people.
Oct–Nov 1974	The IRA carries out six other bombing attacks in England.
27 November 1974	Home Secretary Roy Jenkins introduces Prevention of Terrorism Bill.
29 November 1974	Prevention of Terrorism Act becomes law (after five-minute passage through the House of Lords).
2 December 1974	Giuseppe Conlon sets off from Belfast to London. Arrives at our house the following day.
3 December 1974	Paddy and I, our three sons, Vincent, John and Patrick, Giuseppe Conlon, my brother Sean and a visitor to our house Pat O'Neil, all arrested when the police come to our house on Third Avenue.
7 December 1974	I am charged with murder.

8 December 1974	With Carole Richardson, I am transferred from police cells to Brixton prison in London.
24 February 1975	Murder charge against me dropped. I am charged instead with possession of nitro-glycerine.
	My sons Vincent and Patrick re-arrested and also charged with possession of nitro-glycerine.
April 1975	I am released on bail awaiting trial.
22 October 1975	Guildford Four convicted of murder. Each sentenced to life imprisonment.
12 January 1976	Trial of Maguire Seven opens at Old Bailey, London.
3 March 1976	Maguire Seven found guilty of possession of nitro-glycerine.
	Paddy and I sentenced to fourteen years' imprisonment. Giuseppe Conlon, Sean Smyth and Pat O'Neil twelve years; Vincent Maguire five years; Patrick Maguire four years.
4 March 1976	I am transferred from London to Durham prison in the north of England.
29 July 1977	Our appeal is rejected at Old Bailey.
20 August 1977	Son John marries.
March 1979	Patrick Maguire released from prison.
October 1979	Vincent Maguire released.
23 January 1980	Giuseppe Conlon dies.
31 May 1982	Pope John Paul II, on visit to Manchester in north of England, refers to prisoners, 'innocent or guilty.'
July 1982	Vincent marries.
December 1983	Both Paddy and I are 'decategorized,' meaning that we are no longer classed as 'Category A high security' prisoners and no longer must be accompanied by two officers at all times.

173

February 1984	Paddy is released from jail while I remain a prisoner.
22 February 1985	I am released from prison, the last of the Maguire Seven to be freed.
24 February 1985	On a visit to Belfast with Paddy, I am re-united with my father. He dies two weeks later.
13 May 1985	Irish television's programme on the Maguire case shown on Britain's Channel 4.
17 May 1985	The House of Lords debates the Maguire case, initiated by Lord Fitt.
January 1986	Four hundred Members of Parliament signed 'Motion 280: Miscarriage of Justice' calling on the Home Secretary to initiate a review of our convictions.
13 October 1986	Robert Kee's book *Trial and Error* published. Cardinal Hume and others write to *The Times* following publication.
23 July 1987	Cardinal Hume leads delegation to the Home Secretary, Douglas Hurd.
October 1989	Sir John May appointed to lead investigation into the convictions of the Maguire Seven.
December 1989	Verdicts on Guildford Four quashed and they are released immediately.
12 July 1990	Sir John May produces 'interim' report. Home Secretary refers case to Court of Appeal again.
May–June 1991	Maguire Seven appeal held. On 26 June the 1976 convictions of having handled explosives were quashed.
December 1992	Sir John May, after producing his report on the Maguire Seven case, says on television that ours is the worst miscarriage of justice he has ever seen.
December 1993	The film *In the Name of the Father* premièred in Ireland.
30 June 1994	Sir John May publishes his final report on the Guildford and Woolwich bombings.

GLOSSARY

The Balcombe Street Gang
An infamous IRA unit who confessed at their trial in 1977 to having carried out the Guildford bombings.

Birmingham Six
Hugh Callaghan, Patrick Hill, Gerry Hunter, Richard McIlkenny, William Power and John Walker were tried and wrongly convicted of bombings in Birmingham on November 21, 1974, which killed 21 people and injured 168 others.

Gillespie sisters
Anne and Eileen Gillespie, two sisters from Ireland who were working in England in the 1970s, were convicted of conspiracy in 1974. Throughout their imprisonment they considered themselves political prisoners and I think they rather pitied me for what they thought was my naive belief that under the British system justice would eventually prevail and our names would be cleared. They returned to live in their native Ireland and published a book in Irish and English describing their ordeal in prison.

Guildford Four
Paul Hill, Gerard Conlon, Patrick Armstrong and Carole Richardson, who were tried and wrongly convicted of bombing the two pubs in Guildford on October 5, 1974, which killed five people and injured many others.

Motion 280: Miscarriage of Justice
In January 1986, Four hundred Members of Parliament signed Motion 280: Miscarriage of Justice, calling on the Home Secretary to initiate a review of the convictions of the Maguire Seven. They

noted the widespread belief in the country that the Maguire Seven were "entirely innocent of the crime with which they were charged."

The Old Bailey
The Central Criminal Court in London.

Prevention of Terrorism Act 1974
Rushed through parliament in just two days in November 1974, this emergency legislation, in reaction to the IRA bombing campaign in England, introduced what the then Home Secretary Roy Jenkins admitted were "draconian measures, unprecedented in peacetime." These included giving the police power to arrest and detain suspected terrorists for up to 48 hours or for up to seven days with the Home Secretary's authority.

Price sisters
Marion and Dolours Price were tried and convicted of carrying out car bombings in London during 1972.

Judith Ward
At the time of the Guildford bombings, the trial was taking place of Judith Ward, accused of participating in the so-called M62 bombing, where a coach transporting military personnel was blown up on the motorway. As well as nine soldiers, a mother and her two children were killed. Judith was sentenced to thirty years' imprisonment. This conviction was quashed in 1989, after she had spent fifteen years in Durham prison's infamous 'H' wing.

Warrington bombing
In December 1992, an IRA bomb attack on the northern English town of Warrington killed two young children.

The IRA: A History
Tim Pat Coogan
$27.95 hardcover, $16.95 paperback

'...the standard reference work on the subject...' *The New York Times*

'No student of Irish history can afford to ignore this book. No scholar is likely to improve upon it...A fascinating book, of the greatest possible value to us all.' *The Times Literary Supplement*

The Man Who Made Ireland: The Life and Death of Michael Collins
Tim Pat Coogan
$24.95 hardcover, $14.95 paperback

'Superb...this will be a hard Life to beat.' *The Times Literary Supplement*

'Thanks to *The Man Who Made Ireland*, readers here can get the full story of this good-humoured patriot...[a] heroic account.' *The New York Times Book Review*

To order any of the above please call the toll free number or order from the address below. Send payment with order (check, VISA, Mastercard) and include $3 for postage and handling for each order.

Roberts Rinehart publishes a number of titles of Irish interest. To receive further information and to be put on our mailing list, please write to us or telephone the toll free number below.

Roberts Rinehart Publishers
P. O. Box 666
Niwot, Colorado 80544

1 800 352 1985